P9-DFX-417

HISTORICAL BREAD TIDBITS

- Neolithic people discovered wild grain as a food source; they crushed it between stones, mixed it with water to form dough, and baked it on hot stones near an open fire.

- Prehistoric bread was hard as rock, quite tasteless, full of grit, stones, and ashes, but nevertheless edible and filling.

- Early cultivation of wild grains has been attributed to the Babylonians and Sumerians. By 3000 B.C. they were harvesting wheat and barley for bread making.

- Bread made by the Sumerians around 3000 B.C. was so tough and heavy that it actually wore down the teeth.

Recipes for bread featured on the previous page are:
Crunchy Onion Loaf, Page 48
Pumpkin Bread Delight, Pages 42-43

BLUE RIBBON BREADS
by Mary Ward
and Carol Stine

Photograpy by Barney Taxel

Art direction, book and cover design by Donna Jean Morris

The Library of Congress Cataloging in Publication Data

Ward, Mary and Carol Stine
        Blue Ribbon Breads

Includes Index
       1. Bread Baking   2. Bread History and Trivia
ISBN 0-9621523-1-5   89-095715

First Printing, October, 1989
Second Printing, June, 1996

Printed by Fortran Printing Inc., Cleveland, Ohio

Color Separations by Fortran Printing, Inc., Cleveland, Ohio

Typesetting by Typemasters, Inc., Cleveland, Ohio

Design by Donna Jean Morris
Copy editing by Meredith Holmes, Donna Jean Morris, and Mary Ward
Indexing by Mary Ward
Research by Laura Taxel

Photography by Barney Taxel & Co.
Art Direction by Donna Jean Morris
Food Styling by Mary Ward and Wendy Ward
Props Styling by Barbara Naughton and Carol Stine

Kitchen Testing by WJW & Associates

Published by Hodgson Mill, Inc. Teutopolis, Ill. 62467

C O N T E N T S

CONTENTS

This book has become reality because of the efforts of Rick Siemer, of Siemer Milling, and Donna Jean Morris, the designer and editor of Blue Ribbon Breads. *Thank you both. Thanks also to my daughter (and assistant), Wendy, and to the bread eaters in my family: my mother, my in-laws, my husband, Joe, and my sons, Jon and Bob.*

Mary Ward

I dedicate this book to my husband, Phil, for his patience, understanding, advice, and willingness to try anything. Special thanks to my mother, Elsie, and my mother-in-law, Angela, for all their encouragement; and to my children, Laurie and Andy, for their support.

Carol Stine

INTRODUCTION

You've always thought making bread would be fun and rewarding. Now you've decided to try it. An excellent decision. Bread making is fun, it's certainly rewarding, and it's a lot easier than you might think.

People have been making bread for a very long time. When you picked up this book, you probably didn't know you were embarking on a culinary adventure that would connect you to a tradition thousands of years old. It's common to all lands and all people, and bread is still regarded, the world over, as an essential food. Now more than ever, in these times of mass-produced bread, home-baked bread symbolizes the bounty of the earth, the life of the household, and the pleasures of food shared.

Blue Ribbon Breads, by Mary Ward and Carol Stine, will show you that although bread making has a long history, there is nothing mysterious about it. Nor is it a difficult skill to acquire. *Blue Ribbon Breads* offers more than recipes and baking instructions. There's a glossary of bread making and a chapter on the differences between various grains. Look for interesting historical tidbits, famous quotations, and proverbs about bread. Be sure to read the chapter entitled "Bread Making Tips From Carol Stine's Kitchen," in which an expert bread maker shares her techniques and her wisdom.

Carol Stine is the winner of the bread sweepstakes at the Kentucky State Fair. Once she was a novice like you, but she taught herself how to make bread, and has been practicing this rewarding craft for 20 years.

Mary Ward, co-author and senior editor of *Blue Ribbon Breads*, is a food authority in many areas. She is a nutrition educator, food stylist, food consultant, representative for a variety of food organizations, the author of six cookbooks, and a frequent guest on radio and television shows.

With help from Carol and Mary, a little patience, and lots of wholesome ingredients, you can bake delicious, fragrant bread today.

You'll find that an old saying about bread still holds true: "Fresh baked bread attracts good company and good times." But once you start baking bread, always keep plenty on hand, because, as the French say, . . . "when the bread is eaten, the company says goodnight."

CHAPTER 1

BREAD MAKING TIPS FROM CAROL STINE'S KITCHEN

WARMTH

Yeast is a living organism that must have warmth to grow. You can encourage the yeast to work by making sure that everything it touches—the bowl, the water you dissolve it in, your utensils, and the other ingredients— is warm.

Your attitude is important, too. Remember that you are working with living ingredients. Think warm, think alive, and you will create a hospitable environment for your bread.

Dissolve yeast in water that is warm to the touch. If you aren't sure how to gauge this, use a candy or meat thermometer to measure the temperature of the water. It should be between 110 ° F. and 115 ° F. The yeast won't grow if the water is too hot or too cold. Allow the yeast to rest in the water for five minutes. You'll know the yeast is growing if it gives off a distinctive aroma, and if the mixture begins to bubble.

If the yeast does not grow, check the package to make sure the yeast has not expired. Always buy yeast in the amount you'll need for baking, so you can be assured of using fresh yeast for your bread. If your yeast does not appear to be growing, don't use it. Begin again with a fresh package.

The milk used in most bread recipes must be scalded. You can do this in the microwave or on top of the stove, but don't let the milk boil. Just heat it until bubbles begin to form. Sweeteners, salt, and fat are usually added to the scalded milk. It's important to let milk cool to room temperature before adding it to the yeast. Hot milk can kill the yeast.

If you want a perfect loaf of bread, you must give the dough a warm, draft-free place to rise. This could be a cabinet above your oven, the top of a radiator, a sunny (draft-free) window sill, a spot near a heating duct, or a counter three feet from a wood stove. Be inventive; it's a tradition with bread bakers. In the French countryside, bread was once set to rise overnight in a six foot trough. In the winter, when fires were banked at bedtime, a sheet was spread over the dough, and the lady of the house slept on top of it!

The Normans sometimes set bread dough to rise under the warm blankets of a recently vacated bed. If neither of these methods appeals to you, just preheat the oven to 200° F. for two minutes. Put a pan of water in the bottom of the oven. Turn the oven off and put the bread inside to rise. This is the best method if your house is air-conditioned.

WORKING THE DOUGH

Dough can be mixed by hand, in an electric mixer fitted with dough hooks, or in a food processor that has a dough hook. Kneading by hand produces better results because you can add more flour slowly, to make a soft pliable dough.

In the 19th century, the British naval bakeries turned out huge quantities of bread every day to supply all the ships of the fleet. Kneading was done by a man who climbed barefoot into the vast dough trough and jumped up and down on the dough until it was the proper consistency.

Carol does not recommend this technique, but she does have some helpful suggestions. Use the heels of your hands to fold in the flour and work the dough. Add just a little flour at a time. The less flour you use to feed the yeast, the lighter the bread. In these recipes, you're given a range of flour amounts—two to two and a half cups, for example. If you get the dough to the right consistency with the smaller amount of flour, don't add the other half cup. Your finished loaf will be lighter.

Sometimes you will need more than the suggested amount of flour. Bread dough is affected by weather and the amount of moisture in the flour, as well as by something more subtle about the way you work with it. The important thing is for the dough to have the "look" described in the recipes, usually "smooth and satiny." After you knead the dough about 10 minutes by hand (or four or five minutes by machine) you will notice that it does acquire a smooth, finished look.

RISING

After kneading, the next step is to put the dough in a large, greased bowl. For best results, make sure the bowl is slightly warm. (Remember to think "warm" and alive.") Grease the bowl with vegetable oil, and turn the dough in the bowl so that all its surfaces are greased. This prevents the dough from developing a hard crust. Cover the bowl with a piece of plastic wrap and a warm, damp towel. The plastic wrap keeps the rising dough from sticking to the towel and helps maintain a good level of warmth and moisture in the bowl.

Allow the dough to rise for at least an hour. Check it often, because it might rise too rapidly. If it seems to be swelling fast, knead it down and let it rise again for 30 minutes.

The rising of the bread, more than any other aspect of bread making, symbolizes the rewards of stability and patience. Because you need to be at home, ready for the next step in the transformation of the flour, water and yeast, bread making anchors you in time and place. In our fast-paced, impersonal world, making bread is a wonderful way of taking time to do something well, of savoring the process as much as the product.

After the first rising, gently "punch" the dough down, working out the air bubbles. Often you can hear or feel a slight popping. Some breads require two risings; this produces light, airy loaves. Most recipes for white and whole wheat bread need a second rising in the bowl. Let the dough rest (remember "warm" and "alive") before shaping it, and it will not resist your efforts by springing back. Divide, as instructed by the recipe, and shape.

Bread shapes vary from simple loaves to elaborate braids. The shape of the loaf once revealed the baker's nationality. You can make round loaves, long "French" breads, or free-form farm breads. The shape depends on your ingredients, the suggestions in the recipe, and your own mood on bread baking day. Be creative.

Grease your bread pans with solid shortening, vegetable oil, or no stick cooking spray. Fill the pans with dough according to the recipe's instructions; some breads rise more than others during baking. Cover the pans again, using plastic wrap and a damp towel, and set them in your warm rising place.

BAKING AND STORING

Preheat the oven. If you are proofing the dough in the oven, remove it and place it in the warmest place you can find while the oven preheats. Although each recipe in this book gives you exact baking times, check the bread before the end of the specified time to be sure it does not over-brown. Some ovens are hotter than others, and a few minutes too long in the oven can ruin a good loaf.

When the bread is done, remove it from the pans immediately. Do this carefully with aid of a spatula or knife. Place the bread on racks to cool completely. Do not slice bread until it has cooled completely. There are many superstitions associated with slicing a freshly baked loaf of bread, including one that warns not to cut the bread on baking day. Maybe this was a good way to keep eager hands away from delicious, oven-fresh, bread.

If you plan to freeze some of the bread, be sure it has thoroughly cooled before you wrap and store it. Bread that has been wrapped warm gives off moisture that can cause spoilage.

Carol and Mary hope you find their bread making hints helpful and that you find time to try all the recipes in *Blue Ribbon Breads*. Most of all, they hope you enjoy your own "home-made miracles of bread."

HISTORICAL BREAD TIDBITS

- Using the grain residue from brewers mash for leavening, the Egyptians were the first to produce light, leavened bread.

- The ancient Egyptians considered the rising of the dough to be part of a sacred process, which carried a primal, transforming force.

- Loaves of bread were placed in the tombs of mummified Egyptain Pharaohs to sustain them on their journey to the next world.

- Egyptian workers were paid in bread and beer instead of currency.

Recipes for bread featured on the previous page are (clockwise, starting left center):
Sourdough Bread, Page 97
Swiss Potato Braid, Page 45
Challah, Page 89

CHAPTER 2

GRAIN,
THE ESSENTIAL
INGREDIENT

Milled grain, or flour, is the essential ingredient in bread. As you will discover by reading the recipes in *Blue Ribbon Breads,* there are many varieties of grain you can use in bread making — wheat, corn, oats, rye, and buckwheat. Each grain and each milling process creates a loaf of distinctive texture, taste, and appearance. The recent return to home baking with whole grain flours, and interest in small mills with specialized products has put HODGSON MILL on the map. Flours and grain products from HODGSON MILL are recommended throughout *Blue Ribbon Breads* because they are of superior quality, scrutinized for consistency, and milled using the best methods available to manufacturers today.

The HODGSON MILL has a long and colorful history. Established in the 1880s by the Hodgson family of Gainesville, Missouri, the mill has operated in the heart of the Ozarks for more than a century. In 1969, the Harrington family purchased the original mill, forming HODGSON MILL ENTERPRISES, INC. Besides opening an antique shop, the new owners reaffirmed their faith in the mill and began operating it on a custom basis. As the popularity of naturally milled grains grew, HODGSON MILL decided to create its own line of specialty milled products.

During the 1970s, HODGSON MILL ENTERPRISES, INC. expanded its production facilities to keep pace with the increasing popularity of its milled products. In recent years, the company has continued to respond to the needs of today's health-conscious consumers by reshaping its product line.

In May of 1988, Siemer Milling Co., a 108 year-old family business, acquired HODGSON MILL. Rick Siemer, a member of the fifth generation to run the company, is enthusiastic about the future of HODGSON MILL PRODUCTS. In fact, Siemer Milling's presence in large-scale milling activities guarantees continued growth for HODGSON MILL products.

HODGSON MILL's mission is to provide consumers with superior products that are nutritious as well as tasty. Currently, the HODGSON MILL product line includes:

STONE GROUND YELLOW CORN MEAL
STONE GROUND WHITE CORN MEAL
STONE GROUND WHEAT FLOUR (GRAHAM)
STONE GROUND RYE FLOUR
WHITE FLOUR, UNBLEACHED
BEST FOR BREAD WHITE FLOUR
     (IDEAL FOR ELECTRIC BREAD MAKERS)
50/50 FLOUR
BUCKWHEAT FLOUR
STONE GROUND OAT FLOUR (50/50 STONE GROUND OAT
     FLOUR/UNBLEACHED WHITE FLOUR)
STONE GROUND BROWN RICE FLOUR
STONE GROUND PASTRY FLOUR
PASTA FLOUR (BLEND OF SEMOLINA AND
     EXTRA FANCY WHITE FLOUR)

ACTIVE DRY YEAST
FAST RISING DRY YEAST (50% FASTER; RECOMMENDED
FOR ELECTRIC BREAD MAKERS)
VITA WHEAT GLUTEN YEAST (RECOMMENDED FOR
ELECTRIC BREAD MAKERS)
WHEAT BRAN (UNPROCESSED)
WHEAT GERM
BULGUR WHEAT WITH SOY GRITS
CRACKED WHEAT CEREAL
OAT BRAN HOT CEREAL
WHOLE WHEAT "INSTA-BAKE" BAKING MIX
OAT BRAN MUFFIN MIX
CORNBREAD & MUFFIN MIX
BRAN MUFFIN MIX
STONE GROUND WHOLE WHEAT MUFFIN MIX
BUTTERMILK BISCUIT MIX
STONE GROUND WHOLE WHEAT GINGERBREAD MIX
STONE GROUND WHOLE WHEAT BUTTERMILK PANCAKE MIX
STONE GROUND BUCKWHEAT PANCAKE MIX
JALAPEÑO (MEXICAN STYLE) CORNBREAD MIX
STONE GROUND WHOLE WHEAT MACARONI & CHEESE DINNER
STONE GROUND WHOLE WHEAT SPAGHETTI
STONE GROUND WHOLE WHEAT ELBOW MACARONI

STONE GROUND WHOLE WHEAT LASAGNA
STONE GROUND WHOLE WHEAT MEDIUM SHELLS
STONE GROUND WHOLE WHEAT EGG NOODLES
STONE GROUND WHOLE WHEAT SPINACH EGG NOODLES
STONE GROUND WHOLE WHEAT FETTUCCINE
STONE GROUND WHOLE WHEAT SPIRALS
FOUR COLOR VEGGIE BOWS
FOUR COLOR VEGGIE RADIATORE
FOUR COLOR VEGGIE ROTINI
FOUR COLOR VEGGIE WAGON WHEELS
THREE COLOR VEGGIE NOODLES
15 BEAN SOUP
CORN STARCH
CHOICE BLEND CHILI MIX WITH SPICE PACKET

Many of these products are available at supermarkets, specialty food stores, and health stores. To receive a copy of HODGSON MILL'S 6-color brochure listing all our fine products, write to:

HODGSON BY MAIL
P.O. BOX 430
TEUTOPOLIS, ILL. 62467

OR CALL 1-800-525-0177

WHEAT

Of all the grains, wheat makes the lightest, best rising loaves with the most delicate flavor. Almost all bread recipes call for some wheat flour, including those in *Blue Ribbon Breads*. HODGSON MILL UNBLEACHED WHITE FLOUR, HODGSON MILL BEST FOR BREAD FLOUR, HODGSON MILL STONE GROUND WHOLE WHEAT FLOUR, HODGSON MILL 50/50 FLOUR, HODGSON MILL CRACKED WHEAT, HODGSON MILL BULGUR WHEAT WITH SOY GRITS, HODGSON MILL WHEAT GERM, AND HODGSON MILL WHEAT BRAN all contain wheat flour.

Wheat is rich in gluten, the protein that interacts with yeast to make the bread rise and hold its shape. Wheat flour has always been highly prized for this characteristic. An old Italian proverb says, "He who wants better bread than wheaten, wants too much." For hundreds of years, only the privileged classes could afford wheat flour. Now, of course, high-quality flour is available to everyone. HODGSON MILL, carries a variety of wheat products, white and stone ground whole grain, for all baking needs.

HODGSON MILL UNBLEACHED FLOUR is a blend of hard and soft wheat flours. Suitable for most baking needs, it has not been exposed to chemicals.

HODGSON MILL BEST FOR BREAD WHITE FLOUR is made from high-protein spring wheat. This flour has the greatest quantity of gluten available. Twenty-five to thirty percent of the flour used in bread baking should be bread flour.

HODGSON MILL STONE GROUND WHOLE WHEAT GRAHAM FLOUR is a wheat flour that includes both the finely ground wheat kernel and the bran, which is left coarse and flaky. This flour makes an excellent one hundred percent whole wheat bread and blends well with other wheat flours.

HODGSON MILL 50/50 FLOUR is a blend of HODGSON MILL UNBLEACHED FLOUR and HODGSON MILL STONE GROUND WHOLE WHEAT GRAHAM FLOUR. This mixture is a wonderful substitute for white flour in making light, nutritious whole grain breads.

HODGSON MILL CRACKED WHEAT is a steam, dried wheat that has been cracked into small pieces. Cracked wheat makes an excellent hot cereal. Soaked in boiling water for fifteen minutes, it is a tasty addition to your favorite bread recipe.

HODGSON MILL BULGUR WHEAT with SOY GRITS is a blend of grains in which the wheat has been parboiled, lightly rolled, and mixed with soy grits. The two products make an excellent hot cereal and a tasty addition to yeast breads or quick breads.

HODGSON MILL WHEAT GERM is a flavorful, nutritious supplement that can be added to any bread recipe. The wheat germ is the grain embryo that contains important vitamins and minerals. Wheat germ is highly perishable and must be refrigerated.

HODGSON MILL WHEAT BRAN is the outer layer of the wheat berry, separated in the milling process and very high in fiber. These flakes are used to add fiber to breads and rolls.

CORN

A grain plant native to the Americas, corn was cultivated by the Indians 3,000 years before Columbus arrived in the New World. Incas, Aztecs, Mayas, and North American Indians had corn gods, corn mothers, and corn maidens whom they venerated. It was an important part of the colonial American diet, and was used in corn bread, corn pone, journey cake and 'Injun' bread. Corn meal is made by drying and grinding the whole corn kernel. It is an excellent source of soluble and insoluble fiber. Popular corn products today include corn chips and corn tortillas.

HODGSON MILL STONE GROUND YELLOW CORN MEAL is made from milled yellow corn. It contains all of the natural oils, fiber, vitamins, and minerals originally present in the grain. Since it does not contain any leavening, it's great for making corn tortillas, corn chips, and polenta.

HODGSON MILL STONE GROUND WHITE CORN MEAL is made from white corn. Popular in the South, it may be used in any recipe calling for corn meal and is as nutritious as HODGSON MILL STONE GROUND YELLOW CORN MEAL.

OATS

The oat grain originated somewhere in central Asia and was used primarily as animal food for centuries. Oats, which grow in cold climates, first became a popular food crop in regions of Norway, Switzerland, Ireland, Scotland, and the British Isles where it grew well. Oatmeal, oat cakes, parkin, and haverbread were staples for much of northern Europe. Recently, oat bran has proved effective in reducing blood cholesterol because of its high concentration of soluble fiber. In addition, one serving of oats has twice the protein of a comparable amount of wheat.

HODGSON MILL OAT BRAN HOT CEREAL not only makes a delicious cooked cereal, but also combines well with high gluten flour for delicious quick breads, muffins, and yeast breads. HODGSON MILL OAT BRAN HOT CEREAL is coarsely milled to retain the cholesterol-reducing properties of the oat bran fiber.

HODGSON MILL STONE GROUND OAT BRAN FLOUR is a soft flour that can be used in cake mixes, cookies, breads, muffins, and for meat and vegetable coatings.

RYE

Rye grain, a hybrid of ancient wild grasses, is the hardiest of all the cereal grains and grows well even in poor soils. It has a tolerance for wet and cold conditions and has been popular in Poland, Russia, Germany, and Scandinavia. Rye flour has a flavor and texture associated with peasant breads—dark, earthy, and somewhat sour—but solid and filling.

HODGSON MILL STONE GROUND RYE FLOUR must be blended with wheat flour because it is low in gluten and does not rise well on its own. Used with other gluten flours, it produces delicious breads and rolls, including traditional rye bread and pumpernickel.

BUCKWHEAT

Buckwheat originated in Asia, where it is still a staple. It was brought to Europe from the Middle East by the Crusaders during the 12th Century. In France, buckwheat is still called *bles sarrasin*, Saracen corn. Not a cereal grain, the buckwheat plant is closely related to rhubarb and has more protein than any other grain, but no more calories.

HODGSON MILL BUCKWHEAT FLOUR is used for traditional Russian crepes, or blinis, as well as breads. Because buckwheat has no gluten, bread recipes calling for buckwheat flour should contain four cups of high-gluten white flour for every half-cup of buckwheat flour.

HISTORICAL BREAD TALE

A forgetful Egyptian housemaid left a batch of unbaked dough out in
the hot sun, where by chance, wild, airborne yeast spores settled into it.
Later, to her surprise, she discovered her dough had grown mysteriously
large. After baking this dough, she was even more surprised to discover
an unusually light, soft, loaf of bread. She had unwittingly created
leavened bread.—An Egyptain Legend

Recipes for bread featured on the previous page are:
Whole Wheat Buttermilk Rolls, Page 57
Oat Bran Wheat Rolls, Page 56

CHAPTER 3

YEAST BREADS
by Carol Stine

This chapter includes recipes for breads that have won many blue ribbons at the Kentucky State Fairs. Carol Stine is a Kentucky State Fair Breadmaking Sweepstakes winner and the recipient of many other prizes and awards for breadmaking. Recipes include:

WHITE BREAD

EGG BREAD

HONEY OAT AND WHEAT BREAD

BUTTERMILK OAT BREAD

WHOLE WHEAT BREAD

OAT BRAN WHEAT BREAD

SORGHUM CRACKED WHEAT BREAD

MULTI-GRAIN BRAN BREAD

GRANOLA WHEAT AND BRAN BREAD

GOLDEN RAISIN BREAD

OATMEAL CARROT BREAD

GRANDMA'S OATMEAL BREAD

BANANA OATMEAL BREAD

SWEET POTATO BREAD

PUMPKIN BREAD DELIGHT

OAT BRAN POTATO BREAD

SWISS POTATO BRAID

MASHED POTATO BREAD

CRUNCHY ONION LOAF

CHEESY CORN BREAD

WHOLE WHEAT GRANOLA BREAD

CINNAMON GRANOLA

OAT BRAN GRANOLA CEREAL

White Bread

This is the best recipe to start you off on your exploration of bread baking. Carol's blend of the simplest, most basic ingredients yields a marvelously light loaf. Try baking this bread in three, 1-pound coffee cans. Tied with ribbons, they make delightful gifts.

2 packages (5/16 ounce each) HODGSON MILL ACTIVE DRY YEAST

1/2 cup warm water, 115° F.

1/2 cup margarine, melted

2 cups lukewarm water, 105° F.

1 beaten egg

1/2 cup sugar

1 teaspoon salt

8 cups HODGSON MILL UNBLEACHED FLOUR

solid shortening to coat 1 large bowl and three, 9 x 5 x 3-inch loaf pans

"Music I heard with you was more than music, and bread I broke with you was more than bread."
— Conrad Aiken

Add yeast to 1/2 cup warm water and let stand for 10 minutes.

Combine margarine, 2 cups water, egg, sugar, and salt. Beat until smooth (you may use a mixer). To this, add the yeast mixture and 2 cups of the flour. Mix well, by hand 2 minutes, or with a mixer fitted with a dough hook, for 1 minute. Add remaining flour to make a soft dough. Knead the dough until it becomes smooth and satiny, 10 minutes by hand, or 4 minutes in an electric mixer or food processor fitted with dough hook. Place dough in the greased bowl, turning to coat thoroughly. Cover with a damp towel and allow to rise in a warm, draft-free place for 1 1/2 hours. Knead down and allow to rise until doubled, about 1 hour.

Turn onto a lightly floured surface. Divide into 3 equal portions and let rest for 10 minutes. Grease three, 9 x 5 x 3-inch loaf pans. Shape dough into loaves and put into pans, seam side down. Cover with a damp cloth and allow to rise in a warm, draft-free place until dough rises just above tops of pans, about 1 hour.

Preheat oven to 375 ° F. Bake for 35 to 40 minutes, until top is golden brown. Remove from pans immediately and let cool on racks.

Makes 3 loaves, 12 slices each. Each slice: 129 calories; 1 gm dietary fiber; less than 1 gm soluble fiber; 22 gm carbohydrates; 3 gm protein; 3 gm fat (21% calories from fat); 8 mg cholesterol; 91 mg sodium; 33 mg potassium; 6 mg calcium.

To adapt this recipe for use in an electric bread maker, see Chapter 8, page 152.

Egg Bread

Eggs and finely milled HODGSON MILL BEST FOR BREAD WHITE FLOUR make a rich, golden loaf. This bread will look beautiful braided, glazed with egg yolk, and sprinkled lightly with sesame seeds. Gorgeous!

Add yeast to 1/2 cup warm water and let stand for 10 minutes.

Beat together margarine, 2 cups warm water, salt, sugar, and eggs (you may use a mixer). Add yeast mixture, unbleached flour, and HODGSON MILL BEST FOR BREAD WHITE FLOUR. Knead dough until it becomes smooth and satiny,10 minutes by hand, or 4 minutes in an electric mixer or food processor fitted with dough hook. Put dough in greased bowl, turning to coat thoroughly. Cover with a damp towel and allow to rise in a warm draft-free place for 1 1/2 hours. Knead down and allow to rise for a second time until doubled, about 1 hour.

Turn onto a lightly floured surface. Divide into 3 equal portions and let rest for 10 minutes. Grease three, 9 x 5 x 3-inch loaf pans. Shape into loaves, and put into pans, seam side down. Cover with a damp cloth and allow to rise in a warm, draft-free place until dough rises just above tops of pans, about 1 hour. Brush on egg yolk and sprinkle with sesame seeds, if desired.

Preheat oven to 375 ° F. Bake 35 to 40 minutes, until top is light golden brown. Remove from pans immediately and let cool on racks.

Makes 3 loaves, 12 slices each. Each slice: 134 calories; less than 1 gm dietary fiber; less than 1 gm soluble fiber; 22 gm carbohydrates; 4 gm protein; 3 gm fat (23% calories from fat); 30 mg cholesterol; 96 mg sodium; 33 mg potassium; 7 mg calcium.

To adapt this recipe for use in an electric bread maker, see Chapter 8, page 152.

2 packages (5/16 ounce each) HODSGON MILL ACTIVE DRY YEAST

1/2 cup warm water, 115° F.

1/2 cup margarine, melted

2 cups lukewarm water, 105° F.

1 teaspoon salt

1/2 cup sugar

4 eggs, beaten

6 cups HODGSON MILL UNBLEACHED FLOUR

2 cups HODGSON MILL BEST FOR BREAD WHITE FLOUR

solid shortening to coat 1 large bowl and three, 9 x 5 x 3- inch loaf pans

1 egg yolk beaten with 2 tablespoons water (optional, for glaze)

sesame seeds (optional)

Honey Oat and Wheat Bread

Honey, oat bran hot cereal, and wheat create a sweet crunchy bread. It's sure to become a family favorite, especially when served toasted and spread with marmalade.

2 packages (5/16 ounce each) HODGSON MILL ACTIVE DRY YEAST

1/2 cup warm water, 115° F.

2 1/2 cups lukewarm water, 105° F.

1 1/2 teaspoons salt

1 1/2 cups HODGSON MILL OAT BRAN HOT CEREAL

1/2 cup honey

1/4 cup margarine, melted

6 cups HODGSON MILL 50/50 FLOUR

1 egg

2 cups HODGSON MILL BEST FOR BREAD WHITE FLOUR

solid shortening to coat 1 large bowl and three, 9 x 5 x 3-inch loaf pans

"Beter is half a lofe than no bread." — John Heywood

Add yeast to 1/2 cup warm water and let stand for 10 minutes.

Combine lukewarm water, salt, oat bran hot cereal, honey, and melted margarine. Add 2 cups 50/50 flour and mix well (you may use a mixer). To this mixture add the egg and softened yeast, mix well. Add remaining flours to make a soft dough. Turn onto a lightly floured surface and knead until smooth and satiny, 10 minutes by hand, or 4 minutes in an electric mixer or food processor fitted with dough hook. Put in greased bowl, turning once to coat thoroughly. Cover with a damp cloth and allow to rise in a warm, draft-free place until doubled, about 1 hour.

Knead down. Turn dough out onto a lightly floured surface. Divide into 3 equal portions and let rest for 10 minutes. Grease three, 9 x 5 x 3-inch loaf pans. Shape dough into loaves and put into pans, seam side down. Cover with a damp cloth and allow to rise in a warm, draft-free place until dough rises just above tops of pans, about 1 hour.

Preheat oven to 375° F. Bake 35 to 40 minutes. Remove bread from pans immediately and let cool on racks.

Makes 3 loaves, 12 slices each. Each slice: 133 calories; 2 gm dietary fiber; less than 1 gm soluble fiber; 25 gm carbohydrates; 4 gm protein; 2 gm fat (14% calories from fat); 8 mg cholesterol; 47 mg sodium; 57 mg potassium; 7 mg calcium.

To adapt this recipe for use in an electric bread maker, see Chapter 8, page 152.

Buttermilk Oat Bread

This bread has a heavenly aroma that will fill your entire kitchen. Carol says, "The buttermilk gives it a fresh country flavor. It reminds me of warm, cozy breakfasts in Grandma Stine's kitchen on the farm."

Add yeast to 1/2 cup warm water and let stand for 10 minutes.

Combine buttermilk, sugar, honey, margarine, salt, and oat bran hot cereal. Let rest for 5 minutes. Stir in egg, oat bran flour, and softened yeast. Add HODGSON MILL BEST FOR BREAD WHITE FLOUR and unbleached flour mix to make a soft dough.

Knead until smooth and satiny, 10 minutes by hand, or 4 minutes in an electric mixer or food processor fitted with dough hook. Put dough in greased bowl, turning to coat thoroughly. Cover with a damp cloth and allow to rise in a warm, draft-free place until doubled, about 1 hour.

Knead down dough. Turn onto a lightly floured surface. Divide into 2 equal portions and let rest for 10 minutes. Grease three, 9 x 5 x 3-inch loaf pans. Shape dough into loaves and put into pans, seam side down. Cover with a damp cloth and allow to rise in a warm, draft-free place until dough rises just above tops of pans.

Preheat oven to 350° F. Bake 30 to 35 minutes. Remove bread from pans immediately and let cool on racks.

Makes 2 loaves, 12 slices each. Each slice: 155 calories; 1 gm dietary fiber; less than 1 gm soluble fiber; 27 gm carbohydrates; 4 gm protein; 3 gm fat (71% calories from fat); 12 mg cholesterol; 132 mg sodium; 61 mg potassium; 29 mg calcium.

To adapt this recipe for use in an electric bread maker, see Chapter 8, page 152.

2 packages (5/16 ounce each) HODGSON MILL ACTIVE DRY YEAST

1/2 cup warm water, 115° F.

2 cups buttermilk, room temperature

2 tablespoons sugar

2 tablespoons honey

1/4 cup margarine, melted

1 teaspoon salt

1 1/2 cups HODGSON MILL OAT BRAN HOT CEREAL

1 egg

1 cup HODGSON MILL OAT BRAN FLOUR

2 1/2 cups HODGSON MILL BEST FOR BREAD WHITE FLOUR

2 1/2 to 3 cups HODGSON MILL UNBLEACHED FLOUR

solid shortening to coat 1 large bowl and three, 9 x 5 x 3-inch loaf pans

Whole Wheat Bread

Winner of three prestigious blue ribbons at the Kentucky State Fair, this recipe for wheat bread has been one of Carol's most carefully guarded secrets. After sampling a warm slice, fresh from the oven, you will share the judge's opinion. It's first class in every way!

2 packages (5/16 ounce each) HODGSON MILL ACTIVE DRY YEAST

1/2 cup warm water, 115° F.

2 1/2 cups lukewarm water, 105° F.

1/2 cup sugar

1 1/2 teaspoons salt

1/4 cup margarine, melted

8 cups HODGSON MILL 50/50 FLOUR

1 egg

solid shortening to coat 1 large bowl and three, 9 x 5 x 3-inch loaf pans

"Bread is the staff of life."
— Jonathan Swift

Add yeast to 1/2 cup warm water and let stand for 10 minutes.

Combine lukewarm water, sugar, salt, and margarine. Add 2 cups 50/50 flour and mix well (you may use a mixer). Add egg and softened yeast to this mixture. Add remaining 50/50 flour to make a soft dough. Turn onto a lightly floured surface and knead dough until smooth and satiny, 10 minutes by hand, or 4 minutes in an electric mixer or food processor fitted with dough hook. Put dough in greased bowl, turning to coat thoroughly. Cover with a damp towel and allow to rise in a warm, draft-free place until doubled, about 1 hour.

Knead down. Turn dough onto a lightly floured surface. Divide into 3 equal portions and let rest for 10 minutes. Grease three, 9 x 5 x 3-inch loaf pans. Shape dough into loaves and put into pans, seam side down. Cover with a damp cloth and allow to rise in a warm, draft-free place until dough rises just above tops of pans, about 1 hour.

Preheat oven to 375 ° F. Bake for 35 to 40 minutes, or until golden brown. Remove bread from pans immediately and let cool on racks.

Makes 3 loaves, 12 slices each. Each slice: 116 calories; 2 gm dietary fiber; less than 1 gm soluble fiber; 22 gm carbohydrates; 3 gm protein; 2 gm fat (14% calories from fat); 8 mg cholesterol; 101 mg sodium; 70 mg potassium; 9 mg calcium.

To adapt this recipe for use in an electric bread maker, see Chapter 8, page 152.

Oat Bran
Wheat Bread

A hearty loaf, high in fiber, this bread is both nutritious and scrumptious to eat. Sandwiches made with this bread and your favorite meats, tomatoes, and lettuce will satisfy the hungriest lunch crowd. Yum. Yum.

Add yeast to 1/2 cup warm water and let stand for 10 minutes.

Combine lukewarm water, sugar, oat bran hot cereal, salt, and melted margarine mix well (you may use a mixer). Let sit for 5 minutes to soften the oat bran hot cereal.

Add 2 cups 50/50 flour, mix until well blended. To this mixture, add egg and yeast and mix well. Add the remaining 50/50 flour and HODGSON MILL BEST FOR BREAD WHITE FLOUR to make a soft dough. Turn onto a lightly floured surface and knead the dough until smooth and satiny, 10 minutes by hand, or 4 minutes in an electric mixer or food processor fitted with dough hook. Put dough in greased bowl, turning to coat thoroughly. Cover with a damp cloth and allow to rise in a warm, draft-free place until doubled, about 1 hour.

Knead down. Turn dough onto a lightly floured surface. Divide into 3 equal portions and let rest for 10 minutes. Grease three, 9 x 5 x 3-inch loaf pans. Shape dough into loaves and put into pans, seam side down. Cover with a damp cloth and allow to rise in a warm, draft-free place until dough rises just above the tops of pans, about 1 hour.

Preheat oven to 375 ° F. Bake 35 to 40 minutes, until top is golden brown. Remove bread from pans immediately and let cool on racks.

Makes 3 loaves, 12 slices each. Each slice: 118 calories; 2 gm dietary fiber; less than 1 gm soluble fiber; 22 gm carbohydrates; 3 gm protein; 2 gm fat (15% calories from fat); 8 mg cholesterol; 101 mg sodium; 55 mg potassium; 7 mg calcium.

To adapt this recipe for use in an electric bread maker, see Chapter 8, page 152.

2 packages (5/16 ounce each) HODGSON MILL ACTIVE DRY YEAST

1/2 cup warm water, 115° F.

2 1/2 cups lukewarm water, 105° F.

1/2 cup sugar

1 1/2 cups HODGSON MILL OAT BRAN HOT CEREAL

1 1/2 teaspoons salt

1/4 cup margarine, melted

6 cups HODGSON MILL 50/50 FLOUR

1 egg

1 cup HODGSON MILL BEST FOR BREAD WHITE FLOUR

solid shortening to coat 1 large bowl and three, 9 x 5 x 3-inch loaf pans

"There is not a thing which is more positive than bread." — Dostoevski

Sorghum Cracked Wheat Bread

Old-fashioned sorghum molasses adds a distinctive down home flavor to this easy-to-bake, wholesome bread. Carol has carefully balanced three different flours to produce a richly textured loaf. It's a favorite in the Stine kitchen!

2 packages (5/16 ounce each) HODGSON MILL ACTIVE DRY YEAST

1/2 cup warm water, 115° F.

1 1/4 cups boiling water

1/2 cup milk

1 cup HODGSON MILL CRACKED WHEAT CEREAL

1/2 cup sorghum molasses

1/4 cup margarine

1 1/2 teaspoons salt

4 cups HODGSON MILL 50/50 FLOUR

1 egg

2 cups HODGSON MILL BEST FOR BREAD WHITE FLOUR

solid shortening to coat 1 large bowl and three, 9 x 5 x 3-inch loaf pans

"Acorns were good till bread was found."
— English Proverb

Add yeast to 1/2 cup warm water and let stand for 10 minutes.

Combine boiling water, milk, cracked wheat, molasses, margarine, and salt (you may use a mixer). Cool to lukewarm.

Stir in 2 cups 50/50 flour and mix well. To this, add yeast mixture and egg. Add the remaining 50/50 flour and HODGSON MILL BEST FOR BREAD WHITE FLOUR and mix well to make a soft dough. Turn onto a lightly floured surface and knead until smooth and satiny, 10 minutes by hand, or 4 minutes in an electric mixer or food processor fitted with dough hook. Put in greased bowl, turning to coat thoroughly. Cover with a damp cloth and allow to rise in a warm, draft-free place until doubled, about 1 hour.

Knead down dough. Turn onto a lightly floured surface. Divide in half and let rest for 10 minutes. Oil three, 9 x 5 x 3-inch loaf pans. Shape dough into loaves and put into pans, seam side down. Cover with a damp cloth and allow to rise in a warm, draft-free place until dough rises just above the tops of pans, about 1 hour.

Preheat oven to 375° F. Bake 30 to 35 minutes, until the top is golden brown. Remove bread from pans immediately and let cool on racks.

Makes 2 loaves, 12 slices each. Each slice: 160 calories; 2 gm dietary fiber; less than 1 gm soluble fiber; 29 gm carbohydrates; 5 gm protein; 3 gm fat (15% calories from fat); 12 mg cholesterol; 160 mg sodium; 290 mg potassium; 64 mg calcium.

To adapt this recipe for use in an electric bread maker, see Chapter 8, page 152.

Multi-Grain Bran Bread

This terrific bread is a nutritionist's delight. Hearty and wholesome, it is rich in vitamins and minerals. You'll really want to get your teeth into a slice of it! Bake a double batch and freeze the extra loaves for a rainy day.

Add yeast to 1/2 cup warm water and let stand for 10 minutes.

In a large measuring cup or medium-sized saucepan, heat 2 1/2 cups water and 1/4 cup margarine to 135 ° F. (1 1/2 minutes in the micro-wave or 4 minutes in a saucepan). Pour this warmed liquid in a mixing bowl and add sugar, salt, and oat bran hot cereal. Let this sit for 5 minutes.

Add 2 cups of 50/50 flour and blend well. Add egg and softened yeast and mix well. Add oat bran flour, HODGSON MILL BEST FOR BREAD WHITE FLOUR, and the remaining 50/50 flour to make a soft dough. Turn onto a lightly floured surface and knead until smooth and satiny, 10 minutes by hand, or 4 minutes in an electric mixer or food processor fitted with dough hook. Put dough in greased bowl, turning to coat thoroughly. Cover with a damp cloth and allow to rise in a warm, draft-free place until doubled, about 1 hour.

Knead down dough. Turn onto a lightly floured surface. Divide into 3 equal portions and let rest for 10 minutes. Grease three, 9 x 5 x 3-inch loaf pans. Shape dough into loaves and put into pans, seam side down. Cover with a damp cloth and allow to rise in a warm, draft-free place until dough rises just above pans, about 1 hour.

Preheat oven to 375 ° F. Bake 35 to 40 minutes. Remove bread from pans immediately and let cool on racks.

Makes 3 loaves, 12 slices each. Each slice: 115 calories; 1 gm dietary fiber; less than 1 gm soluble fiber; 21 gm carbohydrates; 3 gm protein; 2 gm fat (15% calories from fat); 8 mg cholesterol; 101 mg sodium; 31 mg potassium; 5 mg calcium.

To adapt this recipe for use in an electric bread maker, see Chapter 8, page 152.

2 packages (5/16 ounce each) HODGSON MILL ACTIVE DRY YEAST

1/2 cup warm water, 115° F.

2 1/2 cups lukewarm water, 105° F.

1/4 cup margarine

1/2 cup sugar

1 1/2 teaspoons salt

1 1/2 cups HODGSON MILL OAT BRAN HOT CEREAL

2 1/4 cups HODGSON MILL 50/50 FLOUR

1 egg

2 cups HODGSON MILL OAT BRAN FLOUR

2 1/2 cups HODGSON MILL BEST FOR BREAD WHITE FLOUR

solid shortening to coat 1 large bowl and three, 9 x 5 x 3-inch loaf pans

Granola Wheat
and Bran Bread

This is one of Carol's newest creations based on her family's favorite granola recipe. Honey, coconut, oats, and nuts blend delicately in this loaf for a surprising treat. It's perfect for those after-school, peanut butter and jelly sandwiches. Be careful! Second helpings might spoil your dinner!

2 packages (5/16 ounce each) HODGSON MILL ACTIVE DRY YEAST

1/2 cup warm water, 115° F.

1/4 cup margarine, melted

1/2 cup sugar

1 1/2 teaspoons salt

2 1/2 cups lukewarm water, 105° F.

1 1/2 cups HODGSON MILL OAT BRAN HOT CEREAL

1 cup Oat Bran Granola Cereal (page 51)

6 1/2 cups HODGSON MILL 50/50 FLOUR

2 eggs

2 cups HODGSON MILL BEST FOR BREAD WHITE FLOUR

solid shortening to coat 1 large bowl and three, 9 x 5 x 3-inch loaf pans

Add yeast to 1/2 cup warm water and let stand for 10 minutes.

Combine margarine, sugar, salt, lukewarm water, oat bran hot cereal, and granola. Let this sit for 5 minutes. Add 2 cups 50/50 flour and mix well (you may use a mixer). Next, add softened yeast and eggs, and blend well. Add the remaining 50/50 flour and HODGSON MILL BEST FOR BREAD WHITE FLOUR to make a soft dough. Turn onto a floured board and knead the dough until it becomes smooth and satiny, 10 minutes by hand, or 4 minutes in an electric mixer or food processor fitted with dough hook. Put dough in greased bowl, turning to coat thoroughly. Cover with a damp towel and allow to rise in a warm, draft-free place for 1 1/2 hours. Knead down and allow to rise for a second time in a warm, draft-free place until doubled, about 1 hour.

Turn dough onto a lightly floured surface. Divide into 3 equal parts and let rest for 10 minutes. Grease three, 9 x 5 x 3-inch loaf pans. Shape dough into loaves and put into pans, seam side down. Cover with a damp cloth and allow to rise in a warm, draft-free place until dough rises just above tops of pans, about 1 hour.

Preheat oven to 375° F. Bake 35 minutes, or until top is golden brown. Remove bread from pans immediately and let cool on racks.

Makes 3 loaves, 12 slices each. Each slice: 225 calories; 3 gm dietary fiber; less than 1 gm soluble fiber; 37 gm carbohydrates; 6 gm protein; 6 gm fat (24% calories from fat); 15 mg cholesterol; 127 mg sodium; 100 mg potassium; 18 mg calcium.

To adapt this recipe for use in an electric bread maker, see Chapter 8, page 152.

Golden Raisin Bread

Raisin lovers beware! Carol's recipe is absolutely loaded with those tempting "fruits of the vine." Serve as French toast topped with fresh strawberries, and your family and friends will sing your praises at the breakfast table.

Add yeast to warm water and let stand for 10 minutes.

Combine scalded milk, sugar, margarine, salt, and orange juice, and cool to lukewarm. Add 2 cups flour and beat by hand until smooth (you may use a mixer). Stir in yeast mixture, eggs, and raisins. Add remaining unbleached flour to make a soft dough.

On a lightly floured surface, knead until smooth and satiny, 10 minutes by hand, or 4 minutes in an electric mixer or food processor fitted with dough hook. Put dough in greased bowl, turning to coat thoroughly. Cover with a damp towel and allow to rise in a warm, draft-free place until doubled, about 1 hour.

Knead down. Turn onto a lightly floured surface. Divide into 3 equal portions and let rest for 10 minutes. Grease three, 9 x 5 x 3-inch loaf pans. Shape dough into loaves and put into pans, seam side down. Cover with a damp cloth and allow to rise in a warm, draft-free place until dough rises just above tops of pans, about 1 hour.

Preheat oven to 375° F. Bake 35 to 40 minutes, until top is golden brown. Remove immediately from pans and let cool on racks.

Blend 4 teaspoons milk with confectioners sugar to make glaze. Drizzle over loaves after they have cooled.

Makes 3 loaves, 12 slices. Each slice: 172 calories; 1 gm dietary fiber; less than 1 gm soluble fiber; 32 gm carbohydrates; 4 gm protein; 3 gm fat (16% calories from fat); 15 mg cholesterol; 121 mg sodium; 111 mg potassium; 22 mg calcium.

To adapt this recipe for use in an electric bread maker, see Chapter 8, page 152.

Dough

2 packages (5/16 ounce each) HODGSON MILL ACTIVE DRY YEAST

1/2 cup warm water, 115° F.

1 1/4 cups scalded milk

1/2 cup sugar

1 stick margarine

1 1/2 teaspoons salt

1 cup orange juice

8 1/2 cups HODGSON MILL UNBLEACHED FLOUR

2 eggs

1/2 cup golden raisins

1 cup dark raisins

solid shortening to coat 1 large bowl and three, 9 x 5 x 3-inch loaf pans

Glaze

1 cup confectioners sugar

4 teaspoons milk

Oatmeal Carrot Bread

Tiny slices of moist, delectable carrots add flavor and character to this hearty bread. The rich, full-bodied texture comes from the combined oatmeal and oat bran hot cereal. Carol often takes this loaf along on picnics. Oatmeal Carrot Bread stays fresh for days.

2 packages (5/16 ounce each) HODGSON MILL ACTIVE DRY YEAST

1/2 cup warm water, 115° F.

1 1/2 cups boiling water

1/4 cup margarine

1/2 cup molasses

1 teaspoon salt

1 cup oatmeal

2 cups HODGSON MILL OAT BRAN FLOUR

2 eggs, separated

2 cups carrots, shredded

2 1/2 cups HODGSON MILL BEST FOR BREAD WHITE FLOUR

2 1/2 cups HODGSON MILL UNBLEACHED FLOUR

1/2 cup oatmeal

solid shortening to coat 1 large bowl and 2 loaf pans or four, 1-pound coffee cans

Add yeast to 1/2 cup warm water and let stand for 10 minutes.

Pour boiling water in a large bowl, add margarine, stirring until it melts. Add molasses, salt, and oatmeal. Let stand for 5 minutes. Add 2 cups oat bran flour and mix thoroughly. Add softened yeast and 2 egg yolks, plus 1 egg white, and mix well. Fold in shredded carrots.

Add 2 1/2 cups HODGSON MILL BEST FOR BREAD WHITE FLOUR and 2 1/2 cups unbleached flour and mix thoroughly. Knead dough until smooth and satiny, 10 minutes by hand, or 4 minutes in an electric mixer or food processor fitted with dough hook. Put dough in greased bowl, turning to coat thoroughly. Cover with a damp cloth and allow to rise in a warm, draft-free place until doubled, about 1 hour.

Knead down dough. Turn onto a lightly floured surface, divide into 2 equal portions for large loaves, or 6 small portions to make gift loaves. Let rest for 10 minutes. Grease two, 9 x 5 x 3-inch loaf pans or four, 1-pound coffee cans. Shape into loaves and put into pans, seam side down. Cover with a damp cloth and allow to rise in a warm, draft-free place until dough rises just above tops of pans, about 1 hour.

Preheat oven to 375 ° F. Brush loaves with egg whites and water and sprinkle with oatmeal. Bake large loaves 30 to 35 minutes, and small loaves 20 to 25 minutes. Remove from pans immediately after baking and let cool on racks.

Makes 2 large loaves, 12 slices each. Each slice: 185 calories; 1 gm dietary fiber; less than 1 gm soluble fiber; 33 gm carbohydrates; 5 gm protein; 3 gm fat (15% calories from fat); 23 mg cholesterol; 122 mg sodium; 279 mg potassium; 58 mg calcium.

To adapt this recipe for use in an electric bread maker, see Chapter 8, page 152.

Grandma's Oatmeal Bread

Breakfast at Grandma Stine's was an event to savor. Carol remarks that "Grandma always mixed molasses into the oatmeal before serving." With fond memories of those country breakfasts, Carol created this hearty loaf. It's a bread you'll savor, too!

Add yeast to 1/2 cup warm water and let stand for 10 minutes.

Combine boiling water, oatmeal, molasses, vegetable oil, and salt. Cool to lukewarm. Stir in 2 cups unbleached flour and mix well (you may use a mixer). To this, add 2 whole eggs and yeast mixture. Mix well. Add the remaining unbleached flour to make a soft dough. Knead the dough until smooth, elastic, and satiny, 10 minutes by hand, or 4 minutes in an electric mixer or food processor fitted with dough hook. Put dough in greased bowl, turning to coat thoroughly. Cover with a damp towel and allow to rise in a warm, draft-free place for 1 1/2 hours. Knead down and allow to rise a second time until doubled, about 1 hour.

Turn onto a lightly floured surface. Divide into 2 equal portions and let rest for 10 minutes. Grease two, 9 x 5 x 3-inch loaf pans. Shape dough into loaves and put into pans, seam side down. Cover with a damp cloth and allow to rise in a warm, draft-free place until dough rises just above tops of pans.

Preheat oven to 375° F.

Brush the loaves with a mixture of 1 tablespoon egg white and 1 table-spoon water, sprinkle with 1/4 cup quick-cooking oatmeal.

Bake 35 to 40 minutes until top is golden brown. Remove immediately from pans and let cool on racks.

Makes 2 loaves, 12 slices each. Each slice: 187 calories; 1 gm dietary fiber; less than 1 gm soluble fiber; 29 gm carbohydrates; 4 gm protein; 6 gm fat (27% calories from fat); 23 mg cholesterol; 132 mg sodium; 120 mg potassium; 21 mg calcium.

To adapt this recipe for use in an electric bread maker, see Chapter 8, page 152.

Dough

2 packages (5/16 ounce each) HODGSON MILL ACTIVE DRY YEAST

1/2 cup warm water, 115° F.

1 1/4 cups boiling water

1 cup quick-cooking oatmeal

1/2 cup light molasses

1/2 cup vegetable oil

1 1/2 teaspoons salt

6 to 6 1/2 cups HODGSON MILL UNBLEACHED FLOUR

2 eggs, beaten

solid shortening to coat 1 large bowl and two, 9 x 5 x 3-inch loaf pans

Coating

1 egg white

1/4 cup quick-cooking oatmeal

1 tablespoon water

Banana Oatmeal Bread

Carol simply loves bananas and honey. In this tasty loaf, she has created an imaginative mix of her favorite ingredients. The bananas add a moist, sweet flavor to the dense, mild oats. It's wonderful toasted and sprinkled with cinnamon.

2 packages (5/16 ounce each) HODGSON MILL ACTIVE DRY YEAST

1/2 cup warm water, 115° F.

1 1/4 cups skim milk

1/4 cup margarine

1/2 cup honey

2 large bananas

1 teaspoon salt

1 cup oatmeal

1 cup HODGSON MILL OAT BRAN HOT CEREAL

1 cup HODGSON MILL OAT BRAN FLOUR

2 egg whites

2 cups HODGSON MILL BEST FOR BREAD WHITE FLOUR

3 cups HODGSON MILL UNBLEACHED FLOUR

solid shortening to coat 1 large bowl and two 9 x 5 x 3-inch loaf pans

Add yeast to warm water and let stand for 10 minutes. In a large measuring cup, combine milk, margarine, and honey. Heat to 135 ° F. (1 1/2 minutes in a microwave or 4 minutes in a saucepan). Pour this liquid into a blender with bananas, and purée.

Pour banana purée into a large mixing bowl, and add salt, oatmeal, and oat bran hot cereal. Mix well (you may use a mixer). Let stand for 5 minutes. Add the oat bran flour and mix well.

Next, add softened yeast and egg whites and mix well. Add HODGSON MILL BEST FOR BREAD WHITE FLOUR and unbleached flour, 1 cup at a time to make a soft dough. On a lightly floured surface, knead dough until smooth and satiny, 10 minutes by hand, or 4 minutes in an electric mixer or food processor fitted with dough hook. Put dough in greased bowl, turning to coat thoroughly. Cover with a damp towel and allow to rise in a warm, draft-free place until doubled, about 1 hour.

Turn onto a lightly floured surface. Divide into 2 equal portions and let rest for 10 minutes. Grease two, 9 x 5 x 3-inch loaf pans. Shape dough into loaves and put into pans, seam side down. Cover with a damp cloth and allow to rise in a warm, draft-free place until dough rises just above the tops of pans, about 1 hour.

Preheat oven to 375 ° F. Bake 35 to 40 minutes, until top is golden brown. Remove bread from pans immediately and let cool on racks.

Makes 2 loaves, 12 slices each. Each slice: 171 calories; 1 gm dietary fiber; less than 1 gm soluble fiber; 33 gm carbohydrates; 4 gm protein; 2 gm fat (13% calories from fat); less than 1 mg cholesterol; 118 mg sodium; 95 mg potassium; 21 mg calcium.

To adapt this recipe for use in an electric bread maker, see Chapter 8, page 152.

Sweet Potato Bread

A honey of a loaf! Sweet potato, honey, and whole wheat flour delicately combine in this rich moist, loaf that's subtly sweet. Try it warm from the oven with cream cheese and a generous sprinkling of crushed walnuts or pecans.

Add yeast to warm water and let stand 10 minutes.

In a large measuring cup or saucepan, combine milk, margarine, and honey. Heat to 135° F. (1 1/2 minutes in a microwave or 4 minutes in a saucepan). Purée mashed sweet potato and liquid in a blender. Pour this purée into a large mixing bowl, add the salt and wheat flour, and mix well (you may use a mixer).

Then add softened yeast and egg whites and mix well. Add the remaining flours to make a soft dough. Turn onto a lightly floured surface, and knead until smooth and satiny, 10 minutes by hand, or 4 minutes in an electric mixer or food processor fitted with dough hook. Put dough in greased bowl, turning to coat thoroughly. Cover with a damp towel, allow to rise in a warm, draft-free place until doubled, about 1 hour.

Knead down. Turn onto a lightly floured surface. Divide in half and let rest for 10 minutes. Grease two, 9 x 5 x 3-inch loaf pans. Shape dough into loaves and put into pans, seam side down. Cover with a damp cloth and allow to rise in a warm, draft-free place until dough rises just above tops of pans, about 1 hour.

Preheat oven to 350° F. Bake until golden brown, about 30 to 35 minutes. Remove bread immediately and let cool on racks. When completely cooled, the bread can be sliced and frozen.

Makes 2 loaves, 12 slices each. Each slice: 141 calories; 2 gm dietary fiber; less than 1 gm soluble fiber; 26 gm carbohydrates; 5 gm protein; 2 gm fat (15% calories from fat); less than 1 mg cholesterol; 120 mg sodium; 121 mg potassium; 27 mg calcium.

To adapt this recipe for use in an electric bread maker, see Chapter 8, page 152.

2 packages (5/16 ounce each) HODGSON MILL ACTIVE DRY YEAST

1/2 cup warm water, 115° F.

1 1/4 cups skim milk

1/4 cup margarine

1/2 cup honey

1 cup cooked sweet potatoes, mashed (fresh or canned)

1 teaspoon salt

3 cups HODGSON MILL WHOLE WHEAT FLOUR

2 egg whites

2 cups HODGSON MILL BEST FOR BREAD WHITE FLOUR

1 cup HODGSON MILL UNBLEACHED FLOUR

solid shortening to coat 1 large bowl and two, 9 x 5 x 3-inch loaf pans

"Whose bread I eat, his song I sing."
— *German Proverb*

Dough

2 packages (5/16 ounce each) HODGSON MILL ACTIVE DRY YEAST

1/2 cup warm water, 115° F.

1 1/4 cups skim milk

1/2 cup margarine

1/2 cup sugar

1 1/2 teaspoons salt

1 cup canned pumpkin

1 1/2 teaspoons cinnamon

1/4 teaspoon cloves, ground

1/4 teaspoon ginger

1/4 teaspoon nutmeg

1 teaspoon orange peel, grated

1 egg, beaten

2 cups HODGSON MILL BEST FOR BREAD WHITE FLOUR

4 to 4 1/2 cups HODGSON MILL UNBLEACHED FLOUR

solid shortening to coat 1 large bowl and two, 9 x 5 x 3-inch loaf pans

Filling

1/2 cup sugar

1 tablespoon cinnamon

Icing

1 cup confectioners sugar

5 teaspoons milk

Pumpkin Bread Delight

Carol enjoys serving this delightful loaf for Sunday brunch. When her guests arrive, they are greeted with the tangy aroma of pumpkin and spices. The aroma and the freshly baked sweet loaves are sure to get a warm reception at your house, too.

Add yeast to 1/2 cup warm water and let stand for 10 minutes.

In a large measuring cup or medium-sized saucepan, heat milk and margarine to 135° F. (1 1/2 minutes in a microwave and 4 minutes in a saucepan). Pour this liquid into a bowl, adding sugar, salt, canned pumpkin, cinnamon, cloves, ginger, nutmeg, and grated orange peel. Let this mixture cool to lukewarm. Add egg.

Add 2 cups HODGSON MILL BEST FOR BREAD WHITE FLOUR and mix thoroughly (you may use a mixer). Fold in yeast and unbleached flour to make a soft dough. Knead until smooth and satiny, 10 minutes by hand, or 4 minutes in an electric mixer or food processor fitted with dough hook. Place in greased bowl, turning to coat thoroughly. Cover with a damp towel and allow to rise in a warm, draft-free place until doubled, about 1 hour.

Combine sugar and cinnamon to make filling.

Knead down dough. Turn onto a lightly floured surface, divide into 2 equal portions, and let rest for 10 minutes. Grease two, 9 x 5 x 3-inch loaf pans.

Continued on next page

Pumpkin
Bread Delight

Continued from previous page

Roll out half the dough into a rectangle 15 x 7 inches and sprinkle half with the filling. Roll up, starting at the smaller edge. Seal the edge and place the seam on the bottom of your loaf pan; tuck in ends. Repeat with rest of dough. Cover with a damp towel and allow to rise in a warm, draft-free place until just above the edge of the pan.

Preheat oven to 350° F. Bake 30 to 35 minutes, until golden brown. Allow to cool.

Combine confectioners sugar with milk and drizzle loaves with icing.

Makes 2 loaves, 12 slices each. Each slice: 201 calories, less than 1 gm dietary fiber; less than1 gm soluble fiber; 36 gm carbohydrates; 5 gm protein; 5 gm fat (20% calories from fat); 12 mg cholesterol; 207 mg sodium; 75 mg potassium; 31 mg calcium.

To adapt this recipe for use in an electric bread maker, see Chapter 8, page 152.

" . . . a jug of wine, a loaf of bread, and Thou."
— Omar Khayyam

Oat Bran
Potato Bread

It might surprise you to discover that oat bran hot cereal and potatoes make a delicious taste combination. The oat bran hot cereal gives this loaf a dense texture, while the potatoes add a moist firmness. It's also a terrific way to use left-over mashed potatoes.

2 packages (5/16 ounce each) HODGSON MILL ACTIVE DRY YEAST

1/2 cup warm water, 115° F.

2 medium-sized potatoes, cooked and mashed

1 cup potato water

1 cup milk, scalded

1 cup HODGSON MILL OAT BRAN HOT CEREAL

1/4 cup margarine

2 tablespoons sugar

2 teaspoons salt

1 egg, beaten

7 1/2 cups HODGSON MILL UNBLEACHED FLOUR

solid shortening to coat 1 large bowl and three, 9 x 5 x 3-inch loaf pans

"To the hungry, bread; to the sleepy, a bench."
— Italian Proverb

Add yeast to 1/2 cup warm water and let stand for 10 minutes.

Combine potatoes, potato water, milk, oat bran hot cereal, margarine, sugar, and salt. Cool to lukewarm. (You may blend mixture to make it smoother.) Add eggs and 2 cups flour, mix well. Add the yeast mixture and remaining flour to make a soft dough. Turn onto a lightly floured surface and knead dough until smooth and satiny, 10 minutes by hand, or 4 minutes in an electric mixer or food processor fitted with dough hook. Put dough in greased bowl, turning to coat thoroughly. Cover with a damp cloth and allow to rise in a warm, draft-free place until doubled, about 1 hour.

Knead down dough. Turn onto a lightly floured surface. Divide into 3 equal portions and let rest for 10 minutes. Grease three, 9 x 5 x 3-inch loaf pans. Shape dough into loaves and put into pans, seam side down. Cover with a damp cloth and allow to rise in a warm, draft-free place until dough rises just above the tops of the pans, about 1 hour.

Preheat oven to 375° F. Bake 30 to 35 minutes. Remove bread from pans immediately and let cool on racks.

Makes 3 loaves, 12 slices each. Each slice: 123 calories; 1 gm dietary fiber; less than 1 gm soluble fiber; 23 gm carbohydrates; 3 gm protein; 2 gm fat (14% calories from fat); 8 mg cholesterol; 132 mg sodium; 67 mg potassium; 15 mg calcium.

To adapt this recipe for use in an electric bread maker, see Chapter 8, page 152.

Swiss Potato Braid

Carol's family loves Swiss cheese melted on baked potatoes. Inspired by that combination, she created a beautiful loaf that's light as a feather. It looks beautiful too, braided, glazed with egg yolk, and sprinkled with poppy seeds.

Add yeast to warm water and let stand 10 minutes. In a large measuring cup or in a medium-sized saucepan, heat milk and margarine, to 135° F. (1 1/2 minutes in a microwave and 4 minutes in a saucepan on medium heat). Pour this liquid into a blender and add mashed potatoes, potato water, sugar, and salt. Blend for 30 seconds.

Pour into a large mixing bowl and add HODGSON MILL BEST FOR BREAD WHITE FLOUR and mix well (you may use a mixer). Now add the egg and softened yeast and blend by hand. Add unbleached flour to make a soft dough. On a lightly floured surface, knead until smooth and satiny, 10 minutes by hand, or 4 minutes in an electric mixer or food processor fitted with dough hook. Put dough in greased bowl, turning to coat thoroughly. Cover with damp towel and allow to rise in a warm, draft-free place until doubled, about 1 hour.

Knead down. Turn dough onto a floured surface. Divide into 6 equal portions and let rest for 10 minutes. Grease two, 9 x 5 x 3-inch loaf pans.

Roll each portion into a long rectangle, 16 x 4 inches, and sprinkle with 1/3 cup shredded cheese. Roll up rectangle to form a rope. Roll out the remaining portions and repeat. Take 3 ropes and braid together, being careful not to stretch dough. Place in a prepared loaf pan. Cover with a damp towel and allow to rise in a warm, draft-free place until doubled, about 1 hour. Brush with egg yolk and water mixture and sprinkle with poppy seeds, if desired.

Continued on on next page

2 packages (5/16 ounce each) HODGSON MILL ACTIVE DRY YEAST

1/2 cup warm water, 115° F.

1 cup skim milk

1/4 cup margarine

2 medium-sized potatoes, cooked and mashed (1 cup)

1 1/2 cups potato water

3 tablespoons sugar

2 teaspoons salt

2 cups HODGSON MILL BEST FOR BREAD WHITE FLOUR

1 egg

3 1/2 to 4 cups HODGSON MILL UNBLEACHED FLOUR

2 cups shredded Swiss cheese

solid shortening to coat 1 large bowl and three 9 x 5 x 3-inch loaf pans

1 egg yolk blended with 2 tablespoons water (for glaze, optional)

poppy seeds (optional)

Swiss Potato Braid

Continued from previous page

Preheat oven to 375 ° F. Bake for 30 minutes, or until top is golden brown. Remove from pans and cool on racks.

Makes 2 loaves, 12 slices each. Each slice: 161 calories; less than 1 gm dietary fiber; less than 1 gm soluble fiber; 23 gm carbohydrates; 6 gm protein; 5 gm fat (26% calories from fat); 19 mg cholesterol; 315 mg sodium; 99 mg potassium; 89 mg calcium.

To adapt this recipe for use in an electric bread maker, see Chapter 8, page 152.

Mashed Potato Bread

Perfect for sandwiches. Try dusting the loaf with flour just before baking. Carol suggests it's just right for grilled cheese sandwiches. Even better, grill the sandwiches in parsley or basil butter. Anyone for seconds?

Add yeast to 1/2 cup warm water and let stand for 10 minutes.

In a large mixing bowl, combine mashed potatoes, potato water, milk, margarine, sugar, and salt. Put this mixture into a blender and purée until smooth. Pour purée back into the mixing bowl and add eggs and 2 cups unbleached flour. Mix well (you may use a mixer).

Fold in the yeast mixture and the remaining flour to make a soft dough. Knead dough until it becomes smooth, elastic, and satiny, 10 minutes by hand, or 4 minutes in an electric mixer or food processor fitted with dough hook. Put the dough in a greased bowl, turning once to coat evenly. Cover with a damp towel and allow to rise in a warm, draft-free place, for 1 1/2 hours. Knead down, and allow to rise until doubled, about 1 hour.

Turn dough onto a lightly floured surface. Divide into 3 equal portions and let rest for 10 minutes. Grease three, 9 x 5 x 3-inch loaf pans. Shape dough into loaves and put into pans, seam side down. Cover with damp cloth and allow to rise in a warm, draft-free place until dough rises just above tops of pans, about 1 hour.

Preheat oven to 375 ° F. If desired, brush a little water over the loaf and sprinkle with flour. Bake 35 to 40 minutes. Remove bread from pans immediately and let cool on racks.

Makes 3 loaves, 12 slices each. Each slice: 122 calories; 1 gm dietary fiber; less than 1 gm soluble fiber; 22 gm carbohydrates; 3 gm protein; 2 gm fat (14% calories from fat); 15 mg cholesterol; 134 mg sodium; 71 mg potassium; 16 mg calcium.

To adapt this recipe for use in an electric bread maker, see Chapter 8, page 152.

2 packages (5/16 ounce each) HODGSON MILL ACTIVE DRY YEAST

1/2 cup warm water

2 medium-sized potatoes, cooked and mashed (1 cup)

1 cup potato water

1 cup milk, scalded

1/4 cup margarine

2 tablespoons sugar

2 teaspoons salt

2 eggs, beaten

8 cups HODGSON MILL UNBLEACHED FLOUR

solid shortening to coat 1 large bowl and three, 9 x 5 x 3-inch loaf pans

Crunchy Onion Loaf

Crisp on the outside, soft on the inside, and flavored with Parmesan cheese and onion, this loaf is tailor-made for Italian menus. Try slicing it thin, then broiling and spreading generously with garlic-flavored butter or margarine. It's also wonderful as an appetizer with melted cheese on top.

1 (5/16 ounce) package HODGSON MILL ACTIVE DRY YEAST

1/4 cup warm water, 115° F.

1 cup milk

2 tablespoons margarine

1 tablespoon sugar

1 teaspoon salt

2 tablespoons minced onion

1 1/2 cups HODGSON MILL WHITE OR YELLOW CORN MEAL

1 egg

2 tablespoons freshly grated Parmesan cheese

1 1/2 to 2 cups HODGSON MILL UNBLEACHED FLOUR

1 cup HODGSON MILL BEST FOR BREAD WHITE FLOUR

1 teaspoon HODGSON MILL WHITE OR YELLOW CORN MEAL

solid shortening to coat 1 large bowl and baking sheet or baguette pan

Add yeast to the warm water and let stand for 10 minutes.

In a large measuring cup or medium-sized saucepan, heat milk and margarine to 135° F. (about 1 1/2 minutes in the microwave or 4 minutes in a saucepan on medium heat). Pour this liquid into a large mixing bowl. Add sugar, salt, and minced onions. Cool to lukewarm. Add corn meal, egg, Parmesan cheese, softened yeast, and mix well (you may use a mixer).

Add flours to make a soft dough. Turn onto a lightly floured surface, and knead until smooth and satiny, 10 minutes by hand, or 4 minutes in an electric mixer or food processor fitted with dough hook. Put in greased bowl, turning to coat thoroughly. Cover with damp cloth and allow to rise in a warm, draft-free place until doubled, about 1 hour.

Knead down dough. Turn onto a lightly floured surface. Divide dough in half and let rest for 10 minutes. Shape each piece into a long narrow loaf, about 14 inches long and 1 1/2 inches in diameter. Place on pre-pared sheet or in baguette pans and sprinkle with corn meal. Cover with a damp cloth and allow to rise in a warm, draft-free place until doubled, about 45 minutes.

Preheat oven to 350° F. Bake 25 to 30 minutes. Remove from pans and cool on racks.

Makes 2 loaves, 8 servings each. Each serving: 150 calories; 1 gm dietary fiber; less than 1 gm soluble fiber; 27 gm carbohydrates; 5 gm protein; 3 gm fat (17% calories from fat); 18 mg cholesterol; 169 mg sodium;114 mg potassium; 41 mg calcium.

To adapt this recipe for use in an electric bread maker, see Chapter 8, page 152.

Cheesy Corn Bread

Here's great chemistry: corn meal, oat bran hot cereal, and cheddar cheese in a moist, grainy bread. Try it toasted and sweetened with honey, spread with herbed butter, or broiled and served with a green salad. Talk about versatile!

Add yeast to 1/2 cup warm water and let stand for 10 minutes.

In a large measuring cup or a medium-sized saucepan, heat milk and margarine to 135° F. (about 1 1/2 minutes in a microwave and 5 minutes in a saucepan). Pour this liquid into a mixing bowl, and add sugar, margarine, egg, salt, oat bran hot cereal, and corn meal. Let this mixture stand for 5 minutes.

Add HODGSON MILL BEST FOR BREAD WHITE FLOUR and blend well. To this, add egg and yeast, mix well. Slowly add shredded cheese and fold into dough. Add 2 cups unbleached flour, to make a soft dough. Turn onto a lightly floured surface and knead until smooth and satiny, 10 minutes by hand, or 4 minutes in an electric mixer or food processor fitted with dough hook. Put dough in greased bowl, turning to coat thoroughly. Cover with a damp cloth and allow to rise in a warm, draft-free place until doubled, about 1 hour.

Turn dough onto a lightly floured surface. Knead down. Divide into 2 equal portions and let rest for 10 minutes. Grease two, 9 x 5 x 3-inch loaf pans. Shape dough into loaves and put into pans, seam side down. Cover with a damp cloth and allow to rise in a warm, draft-free place until dough rises just above tops of pans, about 1 hour.

Preheat oven to 350 ° F. Bake 35 to 40 minutes. Remove bread from pans immediately and let cool on racks.

Makes 2 loaves, 12 slices each. Each slice: 163 calories; less than1 gm dietary fiber; less than 1 gm soluble fiber; 21 gm carbohydrates; 6 gm protein; 6 gm fat (33% calories from fat); 22 mg cholesterol; 217 mg sodium; 78 mg potassium; 93 mg calcium.

To adapt this recipe for use in an electric bread maker, see Chapter 8, page 152.

2 packages (5/16 ounce each) HODGSON MILL ACTIVE DRY YEAST

1/2 cup warm water, 115° F.

1 1/2 cups milk

1/4 cup margarine

2 tablespoons sugar

1 1/2 teaspoons salt

1/2 cup HODGSON MILL OAT BRAN HOT CEREAL

1 1/2 cups HODGSON MILL WHITE OR YELLOW CORN MEAL

1 1/2 cups HODGSON MILL BEST FOR BREAD WHITE FLOUR

1 egg

2 cups cheddar cheese, shredded

2 cups HODGSON MILL UNBLEACHED FLOUR

solid shortening to coat 1 large bowl and two, 9 x 5 x 3-inch loaf pans

Whole Wheat Granola Bread

Judged first class for several years at the Kentucky State Fair, this marvelous bread has a crunchy texture and a nutty flavor. Carol's unique blending of three flours and granola yields a loaf that brings rave reviews and wins blue ribbons. This one is tops!

2 packages (5/16 ounce each) HODGSON MILL ACTIVE DRY YEAST

1/2 cup warm water, 115° F.

1/4 cup melted margarine

1/2 cup sugar

1 1/2 teaspoon salt

2 1/2 cups lukewarm water

1 cup Cinnamon Granola (page 51)

2 cups HODGSON MILL BEST FOR BREAD WHITE FLOUR

2 eggs

2 cups HODGSON MILL WHOLE WHEAT FLOUR

4 cups HODGSON MILL UNBLEACHED FLOUR

solid shortening to coat 1 large bowl and three, 9 x 5 x 3-inch loaf pans

"Bread is better than the song of birds."
— Danish Proverb

Add yeast to 1/2 cup warm water and let stand for 10 minutes.

Combine margarine, sugar, salt, lukewarm water, and granola mix (you may use a mixer). Allow mixture to sit for 5 minutes to soften granola. Add 2 cups of HODGSON MILL BEST FOR BREAD WHITE FLOUR and mix well. Next, add yeast mixture and eggs. Add whole wheat flour and unbleached flour to make a soft dough. Knead dough until it becomes smooth and satiny, 10 minutes by hand, or 4 minutes in an electric mixer or food processor fitted with dough hook. Put dough in greased bowl, turning to coat thoroughly. Cover with a damp cloth and allow to rise in a warm, draft-free place for 1 1/2 hours. Knead down and allow to rise for a second time until doubled, about 1 hour.

Turn dough onto a lightly floured surface. Divide into 3 equal portions and let rest for 10 minutes. Grease three, 9 x 5 x 3-inch loaf pans. Shape dough into loaves and put into pans, seam side down. Cover with a damp cloth and allow to rise in a warm, draft-free place until dough rises just above tops of pans, about 1 hour.

Preheat oven to 375 ° F. Bake 35 to 40 minutes, until top is golden brown. Remove from pans immediately and let cool on racks.

Makes 3 loaves, 12 slices each. Each slice: 152 calories; 2 gm dietary fiber; less than 1 gm soluble fiber; 27 gm carbohydrates; 4 gm protein; 3 gm fat (20% calories from fat); 15 mg cholesterol; 117 mg sodium; 70 mg potassium; 11 mg calcium.

To adapt this recipe for use in an electric bread maker, see Chapter 8, page 152.

Cinnamon Granola

This recipe is the Stine family's favorite granola. It is the "secret" ingredient in Carol's prize winning Whole Wheat Granola Bread. Have it for breakfast with milk. Or enjoy it as a snack over frozen yogurt.

Preheat oven to 350 ° F.

Combine all ingredients and place in an ungreased 13 x 9-inch pan. Stirring occasionally, bake at 350 ° F. for 15 minutes, until golden brown. Cool thoroughly and store in a tightly covered container in the refrigerator.

Makes fourteen, 1/4 cup servings. Each serving: 88 calories; 1 gm dietary fiber; less than 1 gm soluble fiber; 12 gm carbohydrates; 2 gm protein; 4 gm fat (40% calories from fat); 0 mg cholesterol; 1 mg sodium; 59 mg potassium; 8 mg calcium.

1 1/2 cups oatmeal
1/2 cup coconut
1/2 cup pecans
1/4 cup honey
1/2 teaspoon cinnamon
1/4 teaspoon salt

"Never speak ill of them whose bread ye eat."
— Scottish Proverb

Oat Bran Granola Cereal

A delicious and nutritious cereal that's full of fiber. Carol serves it with milk for breakfast and throughout the day for a terrific snack. It's chewy, crunchy, and bursting with flavor.

1 1/2 cups HODGSON MILL OAT BRAN HOT CEREAL

3 cups uncooked oatmeal

1/2 cup honey

1/2 cup nuts, chopped

1 cup flaked coconut

1/4 cup margarine, melted

Preheat oven to 325° F. Combine all the ingredients and mix well. Spread in an ungreased 17 x 11-inch baking pan. Bake in a moderate oven (325° F.) for 25 to30 minutes or until golden brown. Be sure to stir every 5 minutes so mixture browns evenly.

Cool thoroughly and store in a tightly covered container in a cool, dry place or in the refrigerator.

Makes fourteen, 1/4-cup servings. Each serving: 213 calories; 4 gm dietary fiber; less than 1 gm soluble fiber; 28 gm carbohydrates; 4 gm protein; 10 gm fat (40% calories from fat); 0 mg cholesterol; 46 mg sodium; 104 mg potassium; 13 mg calcium.

"He who has no luck loses his bread in the oven."
—*French Proverb*

HISTORICAL BREAD TIDBITS

- The Romans distributed free bread to their citizens, thus iniatiating the first bread dole.

- Bread bakers were civil servents during the Roman Empire.

- A Roman woman, working all day with a hand mill called a quern, could grind enough flour to produce one day's bread for a family of eight.

- With hundreds of slaves working the bread mills 24 hours a day, the Romans produced 50,000 to 100,000 loaves of bread each day.

Recipes for bread featured on the previous page are:
Banana Sweet Rolls, Page 58
Chocolate Cream Coffee Cake, Page 64

CHAPTER 4

ROLLS, COFFEE CAKES, AND SWEET ROLLS

by Carol Stine

How to make friends: bake some of Carol's rolls and coffee cakes, then invite people over to help you eat them. Better still, take these treats to work with you on Monday. Recipes include:

RICH LIGHT ROLLS

GOLDEN CORN ROLLS

OAT BRAN WHEAT ROLLS

WHOLE WHEAT BUTTERMILK ROLLS

BANANA SWEET ROLLS

PEANUT HONEY ROLLS

SESAME OAT BUNS

OAT BREAD STICKS

CHOCOLATE CREAM COFFEE CAKE

CREAM CHEESE COFFEE CAKE

BRAIDED CINNAMON SWIRL ORANGE BREAD

Rich Light Rolls

Carol's blue-ribbon rolls delight the judges year after year at the Kentucky State Fair. Full of homemade goodness, these soft rolls will just melt in your mouth. For variety, try brushing with a mixture of egg yolk and water, then sprinkling with sesame seeds.

2 packages (5/16 ounce each) HODGSON MILL ACTIVE DRY YEAST

1/2 cup warm water, 115° F.

1 cup milk, scalded

1/2 cup sugar

1/2 cup margarine

2 teaspoons salt

5 to 5 1/2 cups HODGSON MILL UNBLEACHED FLOUR

3 eggs, beaten

vegetable oil to coat 1 large bowl and several baking sheets

Add yeast to 1/2 cup warm water and let stand for 10 minutes.

Combine scalded milk, sugar, margarine, and salt; cool to lukewarm. Stir in 2 cups flour and mix well (you may use a mixer). Add yeast mixture and eggs, mix well. Add remaining flour to make a soft dough. Knead the dough until it becomes smooth and satiny, 10 minutes by hand or 5 minutes in an electric mixer or food processor fitted with a dough hook. Put dough in oiled bowl, turning once to coat thoroughly. Cover with a damp towel and place out of drafts. Allow to rise in a warm, draft-free place until doubled, about 2 hours.

Turn dough onto lightly floured surface and roll into 1-inch balls, or your favorite shape, and arrange on prepared baking sheets. Cover with a damp towel and allow to rise in a warm, draft-free place until doubled, about 1 hour.

Preheat oven to 375° F. Bake 10 minutes, or until rolls are lightly browned.

Makes 36 rolls. Each roll: 107 calories; less than 1 gm dietary fiber; less than 1 gm soluble fiber; 17 gm carbohydrates; 3 gm protein; 3 gm fat (27% calories from fat); 23 mg cholesterol; 152 mg sodium; 41 mg potassium; 15 mg calcium.

"It sells like hot bread."
— Danish Proverb

Golden Corn Rolls

These yeasted corn rolls have the moist sweetness of dinner rolls and the grainy, satisfying texture of corn bread. They complement a dinner entree or soup and salad. Corn rolls may also be split, lightly browned, and spread with herb butter.

Add yeast to warm water and let stand for 10 minutes.

In a measuring cup or saucepan, combine margarine and milk to 135° F. (1 1/2 minutes in a microwave or 4 minutes in a saucepan on medium heat). Pour this mixture into a large mixing bowl and add corn meal, sugar, and salt (you may use a mixer). Let cool to lukewarm. Beat the egg and yeast together and add to the corn meal mixture. Cover and allow to rise until bubbly, about 1 1/2 hours.

Stir down the mixture and slowly add 2 cups of flour, mixing well. Add the remaining flour to make a soft dough. Turn onto a lightly floured surface, knead dough until smooth, about 10 minutes by hand or 4 minutes in an electric mixer or food processor fitted with a dough hook. Put dough in oiled bowl, turning once to coat thoroughly. Cover with a damp cloth and allow to rise in a warm, draft-free place until doubled, about 1 hour.

Knead down. Turn onto a lightly floured surface. Let rest for 10 minutes. Shape into 2 inch balls, form each ball into a 4 inch roll, tapering ends. Spray a baking sheet with no stick cooking spray and sprinkle lightly with cornmeal. Set rolls on baking sheet, about 2 inches apart. Cut 3 gashes about 1/2 inch deep across the top of each roll. Cover with a damp cloth and allow to rise in a warm, draft-free place until almost doubled, about 45 minutes.

Preheat oven to 375 ° F. Bake 15 to 20 minutes, until golden brown.

1 package (5/16 ounce) HODGSON MILL ACTIVE DRY YEAST

1/4 cup warm water, 115° F.

1/2 cup margarine

1 1/2 cups skim milk

1/2 cup HODGSON MILL WHITE OR YELLOW CORN MEAL

1/2 cup sugar

1 teaspoon salt

1 egg

5 cups HODGSON MILL UNBLEACHED FLOUR

vegetable oil to coat a large bowl

no stick cooking spray

additional corn meal for sprinkling on baking sheets

"Give the birds crumbs; God gives you loaves."
— *English Proverb*

Makes 20 rolls. Each roll: 187 calories; less than 1 gm dietary fiber; less than 1 gm soluble fiber; 30 gm carbohydrates; 5 gm protein; 5 gm fat (26% calories from fat); 14 mg cholesterol; 172 mg sodium; 83 mg potassium; 32 mg calcium.

Oat Bran
Wheat Rolls

Hearty and high in fiber, these tasty rolls have a wonderful texture. They're even more tempting glazed with egg yolk and dusted with oatmeal. Oat Bran Wheat Rolls also make terrific sandwiches. Split, and stack with your favorite lunch meat, cheese, lettuce, and tomatoes — whatever strikes your fancy.

Add yeast to 1/2 cup warm water and let stand for 10 minutes.

Combine milk, oat bran hot cereal, sugar, salt, and margarine; cool to lukewarm. Stir in 2 cups 50/50 flour and mix well (you may use a mixer). To this, add beaten egg and yeast mixture and mix well. Add remaining 50/50 flour to make a soft dough. Put dough in oiled bowl, turning once to coat thoroughly. Cover with a damp towel and allow to rise in a warm, draft-free place until doubled, about 1 hour. Knead down and allow to rise for a second time for 1 hour.

Turn dough onto a lightly floured surface. Shape into a ball, cover, and let rest 10 minutes.

Preheat oven to 375 ° F. Cut the ball in fourths, then cut each fourth in 6 wedges. Shape wedges in smooth little balls. Place balls of dough on prepared baking sheet, about 2 inches apart. Snip balls almost to center in 3 places to make cloverleaf rolls. Bake 15 to 20 minutes, until rolls are golden brown.

Makes 24 rolls. Each roll: 143 calories; 2 gm dietary fiber; less than 1 gm soluble fiber; 26 gm carbohydrates; 4 gm protein; 2 gm fat (15% calories from fat); 12 mg cholesterol; 152 mg sodium; 79 mg potassium; 28 mg calcium.

2 packages (5/16 ounce) HODGSON MILL ACTIVE DRY YEAST

1/2 cup warm water, 115° F.

1 1/2 cups skim milk, scalded

1 1/2 cups HODGSON MILL OAT BRAN HOT CEREAL

1/2 cup sugar

1 1/2 teaspoons salt

3 tablespoons margarine

5 1/2 cups HODGSON MILL 50/50 FLOUR

1 egg, beaten

vegetable oil to coat a large bowl and several baking sheets

"Everyone gives bread, but none do it like a mother."
— Italian Proverb

Whole Wheat Buttermilk Rolls

Family and friends alike will love the earthy flavor of these rolls. Butter-milk, whole wheat flour, and oat bran give them a real country taste. Perfect with dinners and just right for sandwiches, these rolls take on that professional look if you brush them with melted butter or margarine before baking.

Add yeast to 1/2 cup warm water and let stand for 10 minutes.

In a medium-sized saucepan or microwave-safe bowl, combine marga-rine and buttermilk. Heat until margarine melts (buttermilk may curdle). Add salt, sugar, oat bran hot cereal, and baking soda to the buttermilk mixture and let stand 5 minutes to soften the oat bran hot cereal.

Add 2 cups whole wheat flour (you may use a mixer). Pour in yeast and 1 beaten egg and mix thoroughly. Add HODGSON MILL BEST FOR BREAD WHITE FLOUR and unbleached flour to make a soft dough. Knead the dough on a floured surface until it becomes smooth and elastic, 10 minutes by hand, or 4 minutes in an electric mixer or a food processor fitted with a dough hook. Put dough in oiled bowl, turning once to coat thoroughly. Cover with a damp towel and allow to rise in a warm, draft-free place for 1 hour.

Knead down dough. Turn onto a floured surface and separate into 4 or 5 small balls. Let rest 5 minutes.

Coat a baking sheet with a thin coating of vegetable oil. Flatten each ball into a circle about 9 inches in diameter. Brush each circle with melted margarine and cut in 8, pie-shaped wedges. Roll each toward the point and place on baking sheet, point-side down.

Preheat oven to 375 ° F. Bake for about 15 minutes, or until lightly browned.

Makes 32 to 40 rolls. Each roll: 116 calories; 1 gm dietary fiber; less than 1 gm soluble fiber; 20 gm carbohydrates; 4 gm protein; 2 gm fat (18% calories from fat); 9 mg cholesterol; 112 mg sodium; 69 mg potassium; 24 mg calcium.

2 packages (5/16 ounce each) HODGSON MILL ACTIVE DRY YEAST

1/2 cup warm water, 115° F.

2 cups buttermilk

1/2 cup melted margarine

1 teaspoon salt

1/2 cup sugar

1 cup HODGSON MILL OAT BRAN HOT CEREAL

1/2 teaspoon baking soda

2 CUPS HODGSON MILL WHOLE WHEAT FLOUR

1 egg

2 cups HODGSON MILL BEST FOR BREAD WHITE FLOUR

2 1/2 cups HODGSON MILL UNBLEACHED FLOUR

vegetable oil to coat a large bowl and several baking sheets

Banana Sweet Rolls

Carol says, "I shared the recipe for these rolls with my mother because she loved the wonderful aroma. Sometimes I think she just bakes them to fill the house with their fragrance!" They taste just as good as they smell.

Dough

2 packages (5/16 ounce each) HODGSON MILL ACTIVE DRY YEAST

1/2 cup warm water, 115° F.

1 cup milk

1/4 cup margarine

1/4 cup sugar

1/2 cup sour cream

1 teaspoon salt

1 cup HODGSON MILL OAT BRAN HOT CEREAL

1 egg

1/2 cup banana, mashed

3 cups HODGSON MILL UNBLEACHED FLOUR

1 1/2 cups HODGSON MILL BEST FOR BREAD WHITE FLOUR

vegetable oil to coat a large bowl and three, 8 x 1 1/2-inch round baking pans

Filling

1/2 cup brown sugar

1 teaspoon cinnamon

1/2 cup sliced almonds

Continued on next page

Add yeast to warm water and let stand for 10 minutes.

In a large measuring cup or medium saucepan, combine milk and margarine. Heat to 135° F. (about 1 1/2 minutes in microwave or 4 minutes in saucepan on medium heat). Pour milk mixture into a large mixing bowl, and add sugar, sour cream, salt, and oat bran hot cereal. Let this mixture sit for 5 minutes to soften oat bran hot cereal. Add egg, mashed banana, and softened yeas. Mix well (you may use a mixer).

Add unbleached flour and HODGSON MILL BEST FOR BREAD WHITE FLOUR and blend to make a soft dough. Turn onto a lightly floured surface and knead until smooth, 10 minutes by hand or 4 minutes in an electric mixer or food processor fitted with a dough hook. Put dough in oiled bowl, turning once to coat thoroughly. Cover with a damp cloth and allow to rise in a warm, draft-free place until doubled, about 1 hour.

Combine brown sugar, cinnamon, and sliced almonds to make filling; mix well.

Knead down dough and turn it onto a lightly floured surface. Divide dough in half and allow to rest for 10 minutes.

Roll out half of the dough into a rectangle 15 x 10 inches, brush with 1 tablespoon margarine and sprinkle filling over the dough. Roll up like a jelly roll, beginning with the long side. Seal the edge. Cut in 1 to 1 1/2- inch slices; put cut side down in prepared pans. Cover with a damp cloth and allow to rise in a warm, draft-free place until almost doubled, about 45 minutes.

Continued on next page

Banana Sweet Rolls

Continued from previous page

Preheat oven to 375° F. Bake about 15 minutes, until golden brown. Remove from pan and cool on racks.

Combine confectioners sugar, milk, and almond extract and mix well. Drizzle glaze over rolls when they have cooled.

Makes 24 to 28 rolls. Each roll: 163 calories; 1 gm dietary fiber; less than 1 gm soluble fiber; 27 gm carbohydrates; 4 gm protein; 5 gm fat (26% calories from fat); 12 mg cholesterol; 109 mg sodium; 85 mg potassium; 32 mg calcium.

Continued from previous page

1 tablespoon margarine, melted

Glaze
1 cup confectioners sugar
7 teaspoons milk
1/4 teaspoon almond extract

"Cheese and bread are medicine to the healthy."
— French Proverb

Peanut Honey Rolls

A peanut-butter lover's delight! These marvelous little sweet rolls are filled with chopped peanuts and iced with a peanut butter glaze. They are tantalizing to look at and so much fun to eat! Serve them for breakfast along with a steaming cup of cappuccino.

Dough

2 packages (5/16 ounce each) HODGSON MILL ACTIVE DRY YEAST

1/2 cup warm water, 115° F.

1 1/2 cups skim milk

1/4 cup honey

1/2 cup peanut butter

1 teaspoon salt

1 cup HODGSON MILL OAT BRAN HOT CEREAL

2 egg whites

2 cups HODGSON MILL BEST FOR BREAD WHITE FLOUR

2 1/2 cups HODGSON MILL UNBLEACHED FLOUR

vegetable oil to coat 1 bowl and two, 8 x 1 1/2-inch round baking pans

Filling

1 tablespoon margarine, melted

1 cup chopped peanuts

Glaze

1 cup confectioners sugar

7 teaspoons milk

2 tablespoons peanut butter

Add yeast to warm water and let stand for 10 minutes.

In a large measuring cup or saucepan, combine milk and honey and heat to 115° F. (1 1/2 minutes in a microwave or 4 minutes in a saucepan). Pour this liquid into a medium-sized mixing bowl. Add peanut butter, salt, and oat bran hot cereal and mix well (you may use a mixer). Let sit for about 5 minutes to soften the oat bran hot cereal. Blend egg whites and yeast into oat bran hot cereal mixture.

Add HODGSON MILL BEST FOR BREAD WHITE FLOUR and unbleached flour to make a soft dough. Turn onto a lightly floured surface and knead until smooth, about 10 minutes by hand or 4 minutes in an electric mixer or food processor fitted with a dough hook. Put dough in oiled bowl, turning once to coat thoroughly. Cover with a damp cloth and allow to rise in a warm, draft-free place until doubled, about an hour.

Knead down. Turn onto a lightly floured surface. Divide dough in half and let rest for 10 minutes. Roll out half of the dough into a rectangle 12 x 8 inches, brush with melted margarine. Sprinkle 1/2 cup chopped nuts over the dough. Roll dough, starting with the long side. Seal the edge, cut into 1 inch slices, and place, cut side down, on prepared pans. Repeat this procedure with the other half of the dough.

Continued on next page

Peanut Honey Rolls

Continued from previous page

Cover with a damp cloth and allow to rise in a warm, draft-free place until doubled, about 45 minutes. Preheat oven to 375° F. Bake about 15 minutes, until golden brown. Remove rolls from pans and cool on racks.

In a medium-sized mixing bowl, combine confectioners sugar, milk, and peanut butter; mix well. Drizzle rolls with glaze when cool.

Makes 24 rolls. Each roll: 205 calories; 2 gm dietary fiber; less than 1 gm soluble fiber; 29 gm carbohydrates; 7 gm protein; 7 gm fat (32% calories from fat); less than 1 mg cholesterol; 133 mg sodium; 143 mg potassium; 31 mg calcium.

Sesame Oat Buns

Perfect for summer picnic sandwiches, these buns are a hearty addition to burgers, lunch meats, or salads. Your family will enjoy the crunchy texture and homemade oat flavor. Be sure to bake an extra batch to freeze for unexpected guests.

2 packages (5/16 ounce each) HODGSON MILL ACTIVE DRY YEAST

1/2 cup warm water, 115° F.

1 1/2 cups milk

1/4 cup margarine

3 tablespoons sugar

1 teaspoon salt

1 cup HODGSON MILL OAT BRAN HOT CEREAL

1 cup HODGSON MILL OAT BRAN FLOUR

2 eggs, divided

2 cups HODGSON MILL BEST FOR BREAD WHITE FLOUR

3 1/4 cups HODGSON MILL UNBLEACHED FLOUR

2 tablespoons sesame seeds

vegetable oil to coat a large bowl and several baking sheets

Add yeast to warm water and let stand for 10 minutes.

In a large measuring cup or medium-sized saucepan, heat milk and margarine to 135° F. (about 1 1/2 minutes in the microwave and 4 minutes in the saucepan on medium heat). Pour this liquid into a large mixing bowl and add sugar, salt, and oat bran hot cereal. Let this stand for 5 minutes. To this mixture, add the oat bran flour and mix thoroughly (you may use a mixer). Stir in the 2 egg yolks and 1 egg white, along with softened yeast, and mix well. Add HODGSON MILL BEST FOR BREAD WHITE FLOUR and unbleached flour to make a soft dough. Turn onto a lightly floured surface and knead until smooth and elastic. Put dough in oiled bowl, turning once to coat thoroughly. Cover with a damp cloth and allow to rise in a warm, draft-free place until doubled, about 1 hour.

Knead down dough and turn onto a lightly floured surface. Shape dough in twenty, 2-inch-diameter balls. Put balls on prepared baking sheets and flatten with hand. Cover with a damp cloth and allow to rise in a warm draft-free place until doubled, about 45 minutes.

Preheat oven to 350° F. Brush buns with beaten white of 1 egg and 1 tablespoon water. Sprinkle with sesame seeds. Bake 12 to 15 minutes. Remove immediately from baking sheets and cool on racks.

Makes 20 buns. Each bun: 194 calories; 1 gm dietary fiber; less than 1 gm soluble fiber; 33 gm carbohydrates; 6 gm protein; 4 gm fat (19% calories from fat); 28 mg cholesterol; 145 mg sodium; 77 mg potassium; 40 mg calcium.

Oat Bread Sticks

The perfect cure for a bad case of the munchies, these bread sticks are terrific for snacking. Sprinkle with sesame seeds, onion salt, poppy seeds, or coarse salt for a savory treat. Try serving with a rich marinara sauce or a zesty cheese sauce. They're great for dipping!

Coat a large bowl and several baking sheets with vegetable oil.

Add yeast to 1/2 cup warm water and let stand for 10 minutes.

Combine margarine, sugar, water, salt, and oat bran hot cereal. Let this sit for 5 minutes. Add 2 cups flour, mix well (you may use a mixer), and then add softened yeast. Add the remaining flour to make a soft dough. Knead the dough until it becomes smooth and elastic, 10 minutes by hand or 4 minutes in an electric mixer or food processor fitted with a dough hook. Put in oiled bowl, turning once to coat thoroughly. Cover with a damp towel and allow to rise in a warm, draft-free place until doubled, about 1 hour.

Turn dough onto a lightly floured surface, separate into 3 balls, and let rest for 10 minutes. Roll each ball into an oblong about 1/4 inch thick. Cut into strips 1/2 inch wide and 6 to 8 inches long. Lay strips carefully on prepared baking sheets.

Preheat oven to 400° F. Brush strips with a beaten white of 1 egg and 1 tablespoon water. Sprinkle with sesame seeds, onion salt, poppy seeds, or coarse salt. Cover with a damp cloth and allow to rise in a warm, draft-free place until not quite doubled, about 30 minutes. Bake 10 to 12 minutes. Cool on racks.

Makes 12 bread sticks. Each bread stick: 132 calories; 2 gm dietary fiber; less than 1 gm soluble fiber; 25 gm carbohydrates; 3 gm protein; 2 gm fat (12% calories from fat); 0 mg cholesterol; 161 mg sodium; 39 mg potassium; 6 mg calcium.

2 packages (5/16 ounce each) HODGSON MILL ACTIVE DRY YEAST

1/2 cup warm water, 115° F.

1 1/2 tablespoons margarine, melted

1 tablespoon sugar

1 1/2 cups warm water, 115° F.

1 1/2 teaspoons salt

1 1/2 cups HODGSON MILL OAT BRAN HOT CEREAL

4 1/2 cups HODGSON MILL UNBLEACHED FLOUR

1 egg white

1 tablespoon water

vegetable oil to coat a large bowl and several baking sheets

"If bread is on the table, then the table is fit for a king." — Russian Proverb

ROLLS, COFFEE CAKES, AND SWEET ROLLS

Chocolate Cream Coffee Cake

The ultimate chocolate fantasy: rich, dark, chocolate dough filled with cream cheese and iced with an almond sugar glaze. It's a show-stopper anytime—breakfast, brunch, or late-night dessert. Serve with a cup of café au lait for a European touch.

Dough

2 packages (5/16 ounce each) HODGSON MILL ACTIVE DRY YEAST

1/2 cup warm water, 115° F.

1 cup milk

1/2 cup margarine

1/2 cup sugar

1 teaspoon salt

1/2 cup unsweetened cocoa

4 cups HODGSON MILL UNBLEACHED FLOUR

2 eggs

1 cup HODGSON MILL BEST FOR BREAD WHITE FLOUR

vegetable oil to coat a large bowl and three, 9- inch pie tins

Filling

1 package (8 ounces) cream cheese

1/2 cup sugar

1 teaspoon vanilla

1 egg, beaten

Glaze

1 cup confectioners sugar

7 teaspoons milk

1/4 teaspoon vanilla extract

1/4 cup sliced almonds

Add yeast to warm water and let stand 10 minutes.

In a large measuring cup or medium-sized saucepan, combine milk, margarine, sugar, and salt. Heat to 135° F. (1 1/2 minutes in a microwave or 4 minutes in a saucepan). Stir in cocoa and 1 cup of unbleached flour and mix well (you may use a mixer). To this, add 2 eggs and the yeast mixture. Now add 3 cups unbleached flour and the HODGSON MILL BEST FOR BREAD WHITE FLOUR to make a soft dough. On a lightly floured surface, knead dough until smooth and satiny, 10 minutes by hand or 4 minutes in an electric mixer or food processor fitted with a dough hook.

Put dough in oiled bowl, turning once to coat thoroughly. Cover with a damp towel and allow to rise in a warm, draft-free place until doubled, about 1 hour.

Meanwhile, in a medium-sized mixing bowl, combine cream cheese, sugar, vanilla, and egg. Mix until well blended. Refrigerate until ready to use.

Roll out dough onto a lightly floured surface. Divide into 3 equal portions and let rest for 10 minutes. Roll each portion into a circle 12 inches in diameter. Place a circle of dough in each prepared pie tin. Spread 1/3 cream cheese filling in the bottom of each circle. Cut the dough that hangs over edge of tin at 1-inch intervals. Fold one piece over the first, continuing around the circle until all pieces are overlapped and folded over the filling. Do not cover. Allow to rise in a warm, draft-free place until doubled, about 40 minutes.

Continued on next page

Chocolate Cream Coffee Cake

Continued from previous page

Preheat oven to 350° F. Bake for 25 minutes.

In a small mixing bowl, blend confectioners sugar, milk, and vanilla to make glaze. When coffee cakes have cooled, drizzle with glaze and sprinkle with sliced almonds.

Makes 3 coffee cakes, 6 servings each. Each serving: 271 calories; less than 1 gm dietary fiber; less than 1 gm soluble fiber; 37 gm carbohydrates; 6 gm protein; 11 gm fat (36% calories from fat); 61 mg cholesterol; 237 mg sodium; 101 mg potassium; 47 mg calcium.

Cream Cheese Coffee Cake

In all modesty, Carol says, " Everyone loves this coffeecake. It's my top blue-ribbon winner and has received honors everywhere." One of the best things about this recipe is that it makes three coffee cakes! Serve one and pack the others in lace-trimmed boxes as gifts. Your friends will be enchanted. Cream Cheese Coffee Cake also freezes beautifully.

Add yeast to 1/2 cup warm water and let stand for 10 minutes.

Combine milk, margarine, sugar, and salt. Cool to lukewarm. Stir in 2 cups of the unbleached flour and mix well (you can use a mixer). To this, add the 2 eggs and the yeast mixture; mix well. Add the remaining unbleached flour to make a soft dough. Knead the dough until it becomes smooth and satiny, 10 minutes by hand or 4 minutes in an electric mixer or food processor fitted with a dough hook. Put dough in oiled bowl, turning once to coat thoroughly. Cover with a damp towel and allow to rise in a warm, draft-free place until doubled, about 1 hour.

Meanwhile, in a medium-sized mixing bowl combine cream cheese, sugar, vanilla, and egg. Blend well and refrigerate until ready to use.

Knead down dough. Turn onto a lightly floured surface. Divide into 3 equal portions and let rest for 10 minutes. Roll each portion into a circle, 12 inches in diameter. Place a circle of dough in each prepared pie tin. Dough should hang over the edges. Spread a portion of the cream cheese filling in the bottom of each circle. Cut the dough that hangs over edge of tin at 1-inch intervals. Fold one piece over the first, continuing around the circle until all pieces are overlapped and folded over the filling.

Do not cover. Allow to rise in a warm, draft-free place until doubled, about 40 minutes.

Dough

2 packages (5/16 ounce each) HODGSON MILL ACTIVE DRY YEAST

1/2 cup warm water, 115° F.

1 cup milk, scalded

1/2 cup margarine

1/2 cup sugar

1 teaspoon salt

5 cups HODGSON MILL UNBLEACHED FLOUR

2 eggs, beaten

vegetable oil to coat a large bowl and three, 9- inch pie tins

Filling

1 package (8 ounce) cream cheese

1/2 cup sugar

1 teaspoon vanilla

1 egg, beaten

Glaze

1 cup confectioners sugar

4 teaspoons milk

1 teaspoon vanilla

1/4 cup sliced almonds

Continued on next page

Cream Cheese
Coffee Cake

Continued from previous page

Preheat oven to 350° F. Bake for 25 minutes.

To prepare glaze, combine confectioners sugar, milk, and vanilla in a small mixing bowl. Drizzle over cakes after they have cooled, then sprinkle with sliced almonds.

Makes 3 coffee cakes, 6 servings each. Each serving: 287 calories less than 1 gm dietary fiber; less than 1 gm soluble fiber; 42 gm carbohydrates; 6 gm protein; 11 gm fat (34% calories from fat); 60 mg cholesterol; 234 mg sodium; 96 mg potassium; 41 mg calcium.

Braided Cinnamon Swirl Orange Bread

This sweet bread is gorgeous as well as delicious. Braided and drizzled with an orange icing, it is a first-class treat. Carol says, "The judges cannot resist this bread. It's always a blue-ribbon winner, year after year." You'll get rave reviews too, when you serve Braided Cinnamon Swirl Orange Bread to family and friends.

Dough

2 packages (5/16 ounce each) HODGSON MILL ACTIVE DRY YEAST

1/4 cup warm water, 115° F.

1 cup scalded milk

1/2 cup sugar

1 1/2 teaspoons salt

3/4 cup orange juice

1/4 cup solid shortening

1 tablespoon grated orange peel (optional)

1 egg, slightly beaten

7 cups HODGSON MILL UNBLEACHED FLOUR

1/2 cup sugar

1 tablespoon cinnamon

vegetable oil to coat a large bowl and two, 9 x 5 x 3- inch loaf pans

Glaze

1 cup confectioners sugar

4 teaspoons orange juice

Add yeast to warm water and let stand for 10 minutes.

Mix together milk, sugar, salt, orange juice, shortening, and orange peel. Beat until smooth (you may use a mixer). Add yeast mixture and egg, stir well. Add the remaining flour to make a soft dough. Turn onto a floured board and knead until smooth and satiny, 10 minutes by hand or 4 minutes in an electric mixer or food processor fitted with a dough hook. Put dough in oiled bowl, turning once to coat thoroughly. Cover with a damp cloth and allow to rise in a warm, draft-free place until doubled, about 1 hour.

Knead down. Turn dough onto a lightly floured surface. Divide into 6 equal portions and let rest for 10 minutes. In a medium-sized mixing bowl, combine sugar and cinnamon, mix well.

Roll each portion into a rectangle, 1/2 inch thick. Divide sugar and cinnamon equally among rectangles of dough. Sprinkle each rectangle with a few drops of water and smooth with a spatula. Roll into 6 long ropes, sealing the edges. Braid 3 ropes together for each loaf, and put in prepared pans. Cover, with a damp cloth and allow to rise in a warm, draft-free place until doubled, about 1 hour.

Preheat oven to 350 ° F. Bake for 30 minutes, until tops are golden brown. Remove from pans and cool on rack. Blend confectioners sugar and orange juice for glaze, and drizzle over warm loaves.

Makes 2 loaves, 12 slices each. Each slice: 200 calories; 1 gm dietary fiber; less than 1 gm soluble fiber; 40 gm carbohydrates; 4 gm protein; 3 gm fat (12% calories from fat); 12 mg cholesterol; 91 mg sodium; 79 mg potassium; 22 mg calcium.

HISTORICAL BREAD TIDBITS

- At least 72 varieties of bread were available in the vast Roman market place, including breads made with cheese, honey, olive oil, wine, or milk.

- Wheat bread was prized by the Romans, and the whitest bread was reserved for members of the aristocracy.

- An ancient Greek poem contains the story of Hermes, the messenger of the gods, who was sent to the island of Lesbos to purchase the whitest flour milled in the ancient world.

- According to Greek mythology, Demeter, the goddess of agriculture, gave humans the gift of bread.

Recipes for bread featured on the previous page are:
Maple Sugar Loaf, Page 84
Apple Carrot Muffins, Page 72

CHAPTER 5

QUICK BREADS AND MUFFINS
by Carol Stine

Simple to make in just a few minutes, these muffins and quick breads are as nutritious as they are delicious. Recipes include:

Sour Cream Muffins

A light, sweet, moist muffin that takes minutes to make. This is Carol's simplest basic muffin and a marvelous way to use your imagination. Try adding 1/2 cup drained raspberries or blackberries for a fresh fruit flavor. Raisins, chopped dried apricots, or chopped dates are also terrific.

2 cups HODGSON MILL UNBLEACHED FLOUR

3 tablespoons sugar

2 1/2 teaspoons baking powder

1 teaspoon salt

1/4 teaspoon soda

3/4 cup skim milk

1 egg

1/2 cup sour cream, light

1/4 cup vegetable oil

Preheat oven to 375 ° F. Prepare 12 muffin tins by lining with muffin papers or spraying with no stick cooking spray.

Mix unbleached flour, sugar, baking powder, salt, and soda in a large bowl and set aside. In another bowl, combine milk, egg, sour cream, and oil. Pour liquid ingredients into dry ingredients, and mix until just blended. Batter will be slightly lumpy.

Spoon batter into muffin tins, filling them 3/4 full. Bake 20 minutes, until tops of muffins are golden brown. Remove from pans and serve immediately or cool on racks.

Makes 12 muffins. Each muffin: 155 calories; 1 gm dietary fiber; 1 gm soluble fiber; 19 gm carbohydrates; 3 gm protein; 7 gm fat (42% calories from fat); 27 mg cholesterol; 270 mg sodium; 64 mg potassium; 49 mg calcium.

"As I brew, so I must bake."
— English Proverb

Blueberry Muffins

Carol keeps a batch of these muffins in her freezer. They are a favorite with her teenagers for after school treats. If you like, substitute cranberries for a festive look and taste.

Preheat oven to 400° F. Prepare 12 muffin tins by lining with muffin papers or spraying with no stick cooking spray.

Sift unbleached flour with sugar, baking powder, and salt into a mixing bowl and make a well in the center. Combine egg, milk, sugar, and oil. Add all at once to the dry ingredients, and stir until the dry ingredients are moistened. Fold in the blueberries.

Spoon batter into muffin tins, filling them 3/4 full. Bake for 25 minutes, until tops of muffins are golden brown. Remove from pans and serve immediately or cool on racks.

Makes 12 muffins. Each muffin: 162 calories; 1 gm dietary fiber; 1 gm soluble fiber; 22 gm carbohydrates; 3 gm protein; 7 gm fat (40% calories from fat); 25 mg cholesterol; 348 mg sodium; 55 mg potassium; 61 mg calcium.

1 3/4 cups sifted, HODGSON MILL UNBLEACHED FLOUR

2 tablespoons sugar

2 1/2 teaspoons baking powder

3/4 teaspoon salt

1 egg, well beaten

3/4 cup milk

1/4 cup sugar

1/3 cup vegetable oil

1 cup fresh or frozen blueberries (drained)

"Do not eat bread when another is standing near without holding out your hand to offer some to him."
— Egyptian Admonishment To Children

Apple Carrot Muffins

This is Carol's most adaptable oat bran muffin recipe. The variations are endless, so feel free to experiment. Begin by substituting bananas or apricots for apples. Then use your imagination for additional ideas.

1 1/2 cups carrots, shredded

1 cup apples, chopped

1 cup HODGSON MILL UNBLEACHED FLOUR

1 cup HODGSON MILL OAT BRAN HOT CEREAL

1 tablespoon baking powder

1/2 teaspoon soda

1/2 teaspoon salt

1/2 cup sugar

1/2 cup skim milk

2 eggs

1 teaspoon vanilla

1/4 cup vegetable oil

1/2 cup pecans, chopped

Preheat oven to 400 ° F. Prepare 12 muffin tins by lining with muffin papers or spraying with no stick cooking spray.

Peel and shred carrots; peel and finely chop apples and set aside.

Mix unbleached flour, oat bran hot cereal, baking powder, soda, salt, and sugar in a large bowl and set aside. In another bowl, combine milk, eggs, vanilla, and oil. Pour the liquid ingredients into dry ingredients and mix until just blended. Fold in apples, carrots, and nuts. Let this mixture sit in the bowl for 5 minutes.

Spoon batter into muffin tins, filling them 3/4 full. Bake for 20 minutes until tops of muffins are golden brown. Remove from pans and serve immediately or cool on racks.

Makes 12 muffins. Each muffin: 164 calories; 2 gm dietary fiber; 1 gm soluble fiber; 17 gm carbohydrates; 3 gm protein; 9 gm fat (50% calories from fat); 46 mg cholesterol; 222 mg sodium; 112 mg potassium; 40 mg calcium.

Sunshine Banana Muffins

Brighten your morning with a batch of sunshine muffins. They have all the ingredients for a healthy, tasty breakfast, including oat bran, bananas, and orange juice. Serve warm from the oven and spread generously with orange marmalade.

Preheat oven to 400 ° F. Prepare 16 muffin tins by lining with muffin papers or spraying with no stick cooking spray.

Mix the oat bran hot cereal, flour, baking powder, baking soda, and salt in a large mixing bowl and set aside. In another bowl, mash banana with fork. Beat in milk, orange juice, egg whites, brown sugar, oil, and orange peel. Stir liquid into dry ingredients, mixing until just blended.

Spoon batter into muffin tins, filling them 3/4 full. Bake for 15 minutes, until tops of muffins are golden brown. Remove from pans and serve immediately or cool on racks.

Makes 16 muffins. Each muffin: 120 calories; 3 gm dietary fiber; 1 gm soluble fiber; 22 gm carbohydrates; 2 gm protein; 3 gm fat (20% calories from fat); 1 mg cholesterol; 222 mg sodium; 107 mg potassium; 27 mg calcium.

2 cups HODGSON MILL OAT BRAN HOT CEREAL

1 cup HODGSON MILL UNBLEACHED FLOUR

1 tablespoon baking powder

1/2 teaspoon baking soda

1 teaspoon salt

1 cup very ripe banana, mashed

1/4 cup skim milk

1/2 cup orange juice

2 egg whites

1/2 cup brown sugar

2 tablespoons vegetable oil

1 teaspoon grated orange peel

Maple Nut Muffins

Old-fashioned real maple syrup is worth using in this delightful recipe. The nuts and the oat bran gives these muffins a crunchy texture, while the bananas make them sweet and moist. Spread with your favorite jam and serve with hot herbal tea. Marvelous!

2 1/2 cups HODGSON MILL OAT BRAN HOT CEREAL

3/4 cup HODGSON MILL UNBLEACHED FLOUR

1 teaspoon salt

1 tablespoon baking powder

1/2 cup banana, mashed

1/2 cup skim milk

3/4 cup real maple syrup or 3/4 cup pancake syrup, plus 1 teaspoon maple flavoring

2 egg whites

2 tablespoons safflower oil

1/2 cup nuts, chopped

Preheat oven to 400° F. Prepare 12 muffins tins by lining with muffin papers or spraying with no stick cooking spray.

Mix oat bran hot cereal, unbleached flour, salt, and baking powder in a large mixing bowl and set aside. In another bowl, mash banana with a fork (makes about 1/2 cup). Beat in milk, maple syrup (or pancake syrup and flavoring), egg whites, and oil. Stir maple liquid into dry ingredients, mixing until just blended, and fold in nuts.

Spoon batter into muffin tins, filling them 3/4 full. Bake for 15 minutes, until tops of muffins are golden brown. Remove from pans and serve immediately or cool on racks.

Makes 12 muffins. Each muffin: 194 calories; 4 gm dietary fiber; 2 gm soluble fiber; 29 gm carbohydrates; 4 gm protein; 7 gm fat (31% calories from fat); 1 mg cholesterol; 262 mg sodium; 104 mg potassium; 35 mg calcium.

"All griefs with bread are less." — *English Proverb*

Yogurt Muffins

*Raisins, nuts, oat bran, and yogurt combine to produce these
hearty muffins. Try serving them with softened cream cheese
or Montrachet for an extra dose of calcium and protein.*

Preheat oven to 400° F. Prepare 12 muffin tins by lining with muffin
papers or spraying with no stick cooking spray.

Mix oat bran hot cereal, unbleached flour, baking powder, baking soda,
salt, and brown sugar in a large bowl. Stir in raisins and set aside. In
another bowl, combine yogurt, milk, vegetable oil, vanilla, and egg
whites. Pour liquid ingredients into dry ingredients and mix until just
blended. Then fold in chopped nuts.

Spoon batter into muffin tins, filling them 3/4 full. Bake 20 minutes,
until muffins tops are golden brown. Remove from pans and serve
immediately or cool on racks.

Makes 12 muffins. Each muffin: 193 calories; 3 gm dietary fiber; 1 gm soluble fiber; 33 gm
carbohydrates; 5 gm protein; 4 gm fat (20% calories from fat); 1 mg cholesterol; 296 mg
sodium; 181 mg potassium; 71 mg calcium.

**2 cups HODGSON MILL
OAT BRAN HOT CEREAL**

**1 cup HODGSON MILL
UNBLEACHED FLOUR**

**2 1/2 teaspoons baking
powder**

**1/2 teaspoon baking
soda**

1 teaspoon salt

1/2 cup brown sugar

1/2 cup raisins

**1 cup nonfat or lowfat
yogurt, plain**

1/4 cup skim milk

**2 tablespoons vegetable
oil**

1/2 teaspoon vanilla

2 egg whites

1/2 cup chopped nuts

Apple Juice Muffins

These hearty muffins are full of fiber-rich oat bran. Chunks of apple, bananas, nuts, and spices create a wonderful texture and an unforgettable taste. They will delight friends and family alike. Serve with apple butter for a down-home treat.

2 1/2 cups HODGSON MILL OAT BRAN HOT CEREAL

1/4 cup brown sugar, packed

1 tablespoon baking powder

1/4 cup chopped nuts

1 teaspoon cinnamon

1 banana, mashed

1 apple, peeled and chopped

1/2 cup milk

3/4 cup frozen apple juice concentrate

2 egg whites

2 tablespoons vegetable oil

1 1/2 teaspoons vanilla

Preheat oven to 425 ° F. Prepare 16 muffin tins by lining with muffin papers or spraying with no stick cooking spray.

Mix oat bran hot cereal, brown sugar, baking powder, nuts, and cinnamon. Combine banana, apple, milk, juice, egg whites, vegetable oil, and vanilla. Pour over dry ingredients and stir. The batter will be soupy.

Spoon batter into muffin tins, filling them 3/4 full. Bake for 15 minutes or until tops of muffins are golden brown. Remove from pans and serve immediately or cool on racks.

Makes 16 muffins. Each muffin: 117 calories; 3 gm dietary fiber; 1 gm soluble fiber; 17 gm carbohydrates; 2 gm protein; 4 gm fat (32% calories from fat); 1 mg cholesterol; 139 mg sodium; 95 mg potassium; 39 mg calcium.

Raisin Wheat Muffins

Carol remarks, "A dear friend inspired me to create this recipe when she asked if I knew of a tasty whole wheat, oat bran muffin." The raisins and molasses make it rich in iron, as well as high in fiber.

Preheat oven to 400 ° F. Prepare 12 muffin tins by lining with muffin papers or spraying with no stick cooking spray.

Mix the oat bran hot cereal, whole wheat flour, unbleached flour, baking powder, brown sugar, salt, soda, and cinnamon in a large bowl and put aside. In another bowl, combine milk, egg, vegetable oil, and molasses. Pour liquid ingredients into dry ingredients and mix until just blended. Fold in raisins and let mixture sit in the bowl for 5 minutes.

Spoon batter into muffin tins, filling them 3/4 full. Bake 15 to 18 minutes, until tops of muffins are golden brown. Remove from pans and serve immediately or cool on racks.

Makes 12 muffins. Each muffin: 161 calories; 3 gm dietary fiber; 1 gm soluble fiber; 28 gm carbohydrates; 4 gm protein; 5 gm fat (23% calories from fat); 26 mg cholesterol; 222 mg sodium; 237 mg potassium; 79 mg calcium.

1 cup HODGSON MILL OAT BRAN HOT CEREAL

1 cup HODGSON MILL WHOLE WHEAT FLOUR

1/2 cup HODGSON MILL UNBLEACHED FLOUR

3 teaspoons baking powder

1/4 cup brown sugar

1/2 teaspoon salt

1/2 teaspoon soda

1 teaspoon cinnamon

1 cup milk

1 egg

2 tablespoons vegetable oil

2 tablespoons molasses

1/2 cup raisins

Hawaiian Muffins

Coconut, pineapple, oat bran, and whole wheat are combined in this exotic creation. Moist and dense, these muffins are a marvelous addition to any entrée. For a variation, sprinkle warm muffins with confectioners sugar.

2 cups HODGSON MILL OAT BRAN HOT CEREAL

1 cup HODGSON MILL 50/50 FLOUR

1 teaspoon salt

1 tablespoon baking powder

1/2 cup shredded coconut

1/2 cup sugar

1 egg

1/4 cup milk

2 tablespoons vegetable oil

1 teaspoon vanilla

1 can (15 1/4 ounces) crushed pineapple

Preheat oven to 400 ° F. Prepare 16 muffin tins by lining with muffin papers or spraying with no stick cooking spray.

Mix oat bran hot cereal, 50/50 flour, salt, baking powder, coconut, and sugar in a large mixing bowl and set aside. In another bowl combine egg, milk, oil, vanilla, and a can of crushed pineapple (including liquid). Pour liquid ingredients into dry ingredients, and mix until just blended. The batter will be soupy. Let mixture sit for 5 minutes.

Spoon batter into muffin tins, filling them 3/4 full. Bake for 20 minutes, or until tops of muffins are golden brown. Remove from pans and serve immediately or cool on racks.

Makes 16 muffins. Each muffin: 106 calories; 3 gm dietary fiber; 1 gm soluble fiber; 15 gm carbohydrates; 2 gm protein; 4 gm fat (33% calories from fat); 18 mg cholesterol; 193 mg sodium; 82 mg potassium; 26 mg calcium.

Corn Meal Muffins

The golden color and crunchy texture of corn have long been Southern favorites. To this traditional recipe, Carol adds the homey flavor of buttermilk. Spread with honey or jam.

Preheat oven to 400° F. Prepare 12 muffin tins by lining with muffin papers or spraying with no stick cooking spray.

Mix corn meal, unbleached flour, baking powder, salt, sugar, and soda in a large bowl and set aside. In another bowl, combine buttermilk, egg, and vegetable oil. Pour liquid ingredients into dry ingredients, and mix until just blended. Let this mixture sit in the bowl for 5 minutes.

Spoon batter into muffin tins, filling them 3/4 full. Bake for 15 minutes or until tops of muffins are golden brown. Remove from pans and serve immediately or cool on racks.

Makes 12 muffins. Each muffin: 140 calories; 1 gm dietary fiber; 1 gm soluble fiber; 20 gm carbohydrates; 3 gm protein; 5 gm fat (34% calories from fat); 1 mg cholesterol; 167 mg sodium; 88 mg potassium; 36 mg calcium.

1 1/2 cups HODGSON MILL WHITE OR YELLOW CORN MEAL

1 cup HODGSON MILL UNBLEACHED FLOUR

1 1/2 teaspoons baking powder

1/2 teaspoon salt

1/4 cup sugar

1/4 teaspoon soda

1 cup buttermilk

1 egg

1/4 cup vegetable oil

"The wholesomest of meats is bread."
— *Welsh Proverb*

Apricot Corn Bread

Carol blends apricots and honey into a corn bread with a wonderfully new taste. Once again, Carol's imagination will entertain your family's taste buds. Serve right from the oven with a cool, crisp summer salad.

no stick cooking spray

1 cup dried apricots, chopped

1 1/2 cups HODGSON MILL UNBLEACHED FLOUR

1 cup HODGSON MILL WHITE OR YELLOW CORN MEAL

1 1/2 teaspoons baking powder

1 teaspoon salt

1/2 teaspoon soda

1/2 cup sugar

1 cup buttermilk

2 eggs or egg substitutes

1/4 cup vegetable oil

1/4 cup honey

Preheat oven to 350° F. (325° F. if using glass pans). Spray a 9 x 5 x 3-inch loaf pan with no stick cooking spray or coat lightly with vegetable oil.

Finely chop the dried apricots and set aside.

Mix unbleached flour with corn meal, baking powder, salt, soda, and sugar in a large bowl. Add apricots. In another bowl, combine buttermilk, eggs, vegetable oil, and honey. Pour liquid ingredients into dry ingredients and mix until just blended.

Spoon batter into loaf pan. Bake 50 to 60 minutes or until a toothpick inserted in the center comes out clean. Cool in loaf pan for 10 minutes. Gently loosen sides of loaf. Turn onto wire rack to cool completely.

Makes 1 loaf, 12 slices. Each slice: 182 calories; 1 gm dietary fiber; 1 gm soluble fiber; 30 gm carbohydrates; 4 gm protein; 5 gm fat (26% calories from fat); 1 mg cholesterol; 270 mg sodium; 187 mg potassium; 41 mg calcium.

Cheesy Quick Loaf

The tang of cheddar cheese is unmistakable in this loaf. It's a quick and easy recipe that you can bake on the spur of the moment. The results will be ever so satisfying. For even more piquant flavor, spread with herb butter.

Preheat oven to 350° F. (325° F. for glass pans). Spray 9 x 5 x 3-inch loaf pan with no stick cooking spray or coat lightly with vegetable oil.

Shred cheese and set aside.

Sift flour with baking powder, salt, and sugar into a large mixing bowl. In another bowl, combine eggs, milk, and vegetable oil. Pour liquid ingredients into dry, and mix until just blended.

Fold in 1 1/2 cups of the cheddar cheese. Place batter in loaf pan, sprinkle with remaining cheese.

Bake 40 to 50 minutes, or until a toothpick inserted in the center comes out clean. Cool in loaf pan for 10 minutes. Gently loosen sides of loaf. Turn out onto wire rack to cool completely.

Makes 1 loaf, 12 slices. Each slice: 202 calories; 1 gm dietary fiber; 1 gm soluble fiber; 19 gm carbohydrates; 9 gm protein; 10 gm fat (44% calories from fat); 66 mg cholesterol; 389 mg sodium; 93 mg potassium; 14 mg calcium.

no stick cooking spray

2 cups cheddar cheese, shredded

2 1/4 cups HODGSON MILL UNBLEACHED FLOUR

3 teaspoons baking powder

1 teaspoon salt

1 tablespoon sugar

2 eggs

1 1/4 cups skim milk

2 tablespoons vegetable oil

"He is as good as good bread." — French Proverb

Vita Loaf

Plenty of apples, carrots, and nuts create a loaf that is full of fiber, moist, sweet, and flavorful, yet low in calories. A terrific appetizer with berries and sliced fresh fruit.

no stick cooking spray

1 1/2 cups carrots, shredded

1 1/2 cups apples, chopped

2 cups HODGSON MILL UNBLEACHED WHITE FLOUR

3 teaspoons baking powder

1 teaspoon salt

1/4 teaspoon soda

1/2 cup sugar

1/2 cup buttermilk

2 eggs

1 teaspoon vanilla

1/2 cup vegetable oil

3/4 cups chopped nuts

Preheat oven to 350° F. (325° F. for glass pans). Spray a 9 x 5 x 3-inch loaf pan with no stick cooking spray or coat lightly with vegetable oil.

Peel and shred carrots; peel and finely chop apples and set aside.

Mix unbleached flour, baking powder, salt, soda, and sugar in a large bowl and put aside. In another bowl, combine buttermilk, eggs, vanilla, and vegetable oil. Pour liquid ingredients into dry ingredients and mix until just blended. Fold in carrots, apples, and nuts.

Spoon batter into loaf pan and bake for 1 hour, or until a toothpick inserted in the center comes out clean. Cool in loaf pan for 10 minutes. Gently loosen sides of loaf. Turn onto wire rack to cool completely.

Makes 1 loaf, 12 slices. Each slice: 264 calories; 2 gm dietary fiber; 1 gm soluble fiber; 30 gm carbohydrates; 5 gm protein; 15 gm fat (26% calories from fat); 46 mg cholesterol; 293 mg sodium; 172 mg potassium; 62 mg calcium.

Sour Cream Loaf

A hint of orange and cinnamon gives this loaf a tempting tang. For brunch, serve with marmalade or jam. Or try it as a light desert with fresh fruit on the side.

Preheat oven to 350° F. (325° F. for glass pans). Spray a 9 x 5 x 3-inch loaf pan with no stick cooking spray or coat lightly with vegetable oil.

Cream margarine and sugar until fluffy. Add eggs, beating well. Then mix in sour cream and orange peel.

Sift unbleached flour with baking powder and gradually fold into cream mixture. Put half of the batter in a greased loaf pan. Combine cinnamon, brown sugar, and nuts to make topping. Sprinkle half over batter in pan. Add the remaining batter, and sprinkle rest of nut mixture on top.

Bake 55 to 60 minutes, or until a toothpick inserted in the center comes out clean. Cool in the pan for 10 minutes. Gently loosen sides of loaf. Turn onto wire rack and cool completely.

Makes 1 loaf, 12 slices. Each slice: 308 calories; 1 gm dietary fiber; 1 gm soluble fiber; 46 gm carbohydrates; 4 gm protein; 13 gm fat (37% calories from fat); 8 mg cholesterol; 287 mg sodium; 113 mg potassium; 64 mg calcium.

Batter

no stick cooking spray

1/2 cup margarine

1 1/2 cups sugar

2 eggs

1 cup light sour cream

1 1/2 teaspoons orange peel, grated

2 cups HODGSON MILL UNBLEACHED FLOUR

3 teaspoons baking powder

1/2 teaspoon salt

Topping

1 1/2 teaspoons cinnamon

4 tablespoons brown sugar

1/2 cup chopped nuts

Maple Sugar Loaf

The aroma of maple is wonderful while this loaf is baking. A streusel topping of nuts, sugar, and cinnamon adds to the aroma. Needless to say, when it's done, it's simply scrumptious. Carol likes to wrap this loaf with a pretty ribbon and give it to her friends. It freezes beautifully, too.

Batter

no stick cooking spray

2 cups HODGSON MILL UNBLEACHED FLOUR

3 teaspoons baking powder

1 teaspoon salt

1/2 teaspoon baking soda

1 cup sugar

1/2 cup buttermilk

1/2 cup sour cream

2 eggs

1/2 cup vegetable oil

1/2 teaspoon vanilla

1 teaspoon maple flavoring

Streusel Topping

3 tablespoons brown sugar

1/2 cup chopped nuts

1/2 teaspoon cinnamon

Preheat oven to 350° F. (325° F. for glass pans). Spray a 9 x 5 x 3-inch loaf pan with no stick cooking spray or coat lightly with vegetable oil.

Mix flour, baking powder, salt, soda, and sugar in a large bowl. In another bowl, combine buttermilk, sour cream, eggs, vegetable oil, vanilla, and maple flavoring. Pour liquid ingredients into dry ingredients, and mix until just blended.

To make streusel topping, blend brown sugar with nuts and cinnamon.

Spoon half the batter into pan and sprinkle with 1/2 streusel topping mixture. Spoon in the remaining batter, and top with the rest of the streusel mixture.

Bake 50 to 60 minutes, or until a toothpick inserted in the center comes out clean. Cool in the pan for 10 minutes. Gently loosen sides of loaf. Turn onto wire rack and cool completely.

Makes 1 loaf, 12 slices. Each slice: 294 calories; 1 gm dietary fiber; 0.5 gm soluble fiber; 36 gm carbohydrates; 5 gm protein; 15 gm fat (45% calories from fat); 50 mg cholesterol; 311 mg sodium; 111 mg potassium; 65 mg calcium.

Date Nut Loaf

Plenty of dates and nuts create a rich, subtle loaf that is a favorite dessert in the Stine home. Spread with softened cream cheese and serve with fresh, sliced apples, peaches, or pears. Luscious!

Preheat oven to 350° F. (325° F. for glass pans). Spray a 9 x 5 x 3-inch loaf pan with no stick cooking spray or coat lightly with vegetable oil.

Mix unbleached flour, baking powder, salt, soda, and sugar in a large bowl. Add the chopped dates and nuts.

In another bowl, combine egg, milk, vegetable oil, and vanilla. Pour liquid ingredients into dry ingredients, and mix until just blended.

Spoon batter into loaf pan. Bake 50 to 60 minutes or until a toothpick inserted in the center comes out clean. Cool in loaf pan for 10 minutes. Gently loosen sides of loaf. Turn onto wire rack to cool completely.

Makes 1 loaf, 12 slices. Each slice: 308 calories; 3 gm dietary fiber; 1 gm soluble fiber; 47 gm carbohydrates; 4 gm protein; 13 gm fat (36% calories from fat); 23 mg cholesterol; 289 mg sodium; 166 mg potassium; 41 mg calcium.

no stick cooking spray

2 1/2 cups HODGSON MILL UNBLEACHED FLOUR

3 teaspoons baking powder

1 teaspoon salt

1/2 teaspoon soda

1 cup sugar

1 cup dates, chopped

1/2 cup nuts, chopped

1 egg

1 cup milk

1/2 cup vegetable oil

1 teaspoon vanilla

Fruit and Honey Loaf

Apricots, dates, apples, a bit of orange, and a dollop of honey are the not-so-secret ingredients of this bread. It's simple to make, and guests will love it. Have it for breakfast with hot Viennese coffee.

no stick cooking spray

1/2 cup dried apricots, chopped

1/2 cup dates, chopped

1 cup apple, chopped

1 3/4 cups HODGSON MILL UNBLEACHED FLOUR

1 1/2 teaspoons baking powder

1 cup graham cracker crumbs

2 teaspoons orange peel, grated

1/2 cup honey

1/4 cup vegetable oil

2 eggs

1/4 cup orange juice

Preheat oven to 350° F. (325° F. for glass pans). Spray a 9 x 5 x 3-inch loaf pan with no stick cooking spray or coat lightly with vegetable oil.

Finely chop dried apricots, dates, and apples and set aside.

Mix unbleached flour, baking powder, and graham cracker crumbs in a large bowl. Add chopped fruit and orange peel. In another bowl, combine honey, oil, eggs, and orange juice. Pour liquid ingredients into dry ingredients, and mix until just blended.

Spoon batter in a greased loaf pan and bake 50 to 60 minutes, or until a toothpick inserted in the center comes out clean. Cool in the pan for 10 minutes. Gently loosen sides of loaf. Turn onto wire rack and cool completely. Freezes well.

Makes 1 loaf, 12 slices. Each slice: 270 calories; 3 gm dietary fiber; 3 gm soluble fiber; 48 gm carbohydrates; 4 gm protein; 7 gm fat (23% calories from fat); 46 mg cholesterol; 144 mg sodium; 230 mg potassium; 28 mg calcium.

HISTORICAL BREAD TIDBITS

- In the Middle Ages, thick slabs of bread called trenchers were used as plates, and often, were the entire meal itself.

- Owning vast tracts of farmland gave feudal lords great wealth and power, enabling them to control grain stores, mills, ovens, and even the bakers.

- The modern word, *lord,* is derived from the Anglo-Saxon word *hlaford,* which meant the landowner who gave out the bread.

Recipes for bread featured on the previous page are:
Focaccia, Page 95
Corn Tortillas, Page 104

CHAPTER 6

INTERNATIONAL BREADS

by Mary Ward

This collection of recipes is from all over the world. The breads are simple to make, yet authentic. They include:

Polenta

Polenta is a staple dish in Northern Italy. We know it as corn meal mush—a hot cereal with a thousand uses. Mary likes to serve polenta with finely grated cheese and a bit of jalapeño pepper to add regional flair. Mama Mia!

no stick cooking spray

1 cup HODGSON MILL WHITE OR YELLOW CORN MEAL

3/4 cup water

3 1/4 cups boiling water

1 teaspoon salt

1 to 2 tablespoons finely chopped jalapeño pepper

1 tablespoon soft margarine

1 cup freshly grated Romano cheese

1/3 cup shredded Provolone cheese

Preheat oven to 350° F. Spray a 1 1/2 quart baking dish with no stick cooking spray.

Mix corn meal with 3/4 cup water in a medium-sized sauce pan. Stir in boiling water, salt, and jalapeño pepper. Cook, stirring constantly, until mixture thickens and boils. Cover and simmer, stirring occasionally, for 10 minutes. Remove from heat; stir until smooth.

Spread 1/3 of the mixture in prepared dish. Dot with 1/3 of the margarine; sprinkle with 1/3 of Romano cheese. Repeat twice. Sprinkle with Provolone. Bake uncovered until hot and bubbly, about 15 minutes.

Makes 6 servings. Each serving: 305 calories; less than 1 gm dietary fiber; less than 1 gm soluble fiber; 20 gm carbohydrates; 18 gm protein; 17 gm fat (50% calories from fat); 50 mg cholesterol; 316 mg sodium; 54 mg potassium; 534 mg calcium.

"Bread and radishes are food for the gods."
— Spanish Proverb

Challah
(Jewish Egg Braid)

This sweet, light bread is usually served at the Friday night Sabbath meal. Very large loaves of Challah are shared at celebrations, such as weddings and bar mitzvahs. Mary seldom uses whole eggs, but the yolk is essential in this recipe. Beautiful to look at, delicious to eat, Challah makes any meal festive.

Spray a large bowl with no stick cooking spray.

In a another large bowl, dissolve yeast in warm water and allow to rest for 5 minutes. Stir in sugar, salt, egg, oil, HODGSON MILL BEST FOR BREAD WHITE FLOUR, and 1/2 cup of the unbleached flour. Beat until smooth. Stir in enough of remaining flour to make a smooth dough.

Turn dough onto a lightly floured board. Knead until smooth and elastic, 5 minutes. Place in bowl and turn to coat thoroughly. Cover with plastic wrap and a wet towel. Allow to rise in a warm, draft-free place for 1 1/2 to 2 hours. Dough will be almost doubled.

Spray a baking sheet with no stick cooking spray. Knead down dough. Divide into 6 equal parts. Roll each part into a thin rope about 12 inches long. Put ropes close together on prepared baking sheet. Braid ropes gently and loosely without stretching them. Tuck ends under braid and brush with vegetable oil. Cover and allow to rise in a warm, draft-free place for 1 hour.

Preheat oven to 350° F. Mix egg yolk and water. Brush dough with egg yolk mixture. Sprinkle with poppy seeds or sesame seeds, if desired. Bake until golden brown, about 30 minutes.

Dough

no stick cooking spray

1 package (5/16 ounce) HODGSON MILL ACTIVE DRY YEAST

3/4 cup very warm water, 115° F.

2 tablespoons sugar

1 teaspoon salt

1 egg

1 tablespoon vegetable oil

1 cup HODGSON MILL BEST FOR BREAD WHITE FLOUR

1 1/2 to 1 3/4 cups HODGSON MILL UNBLEACHED FLOUR

1 tablespoon vegetable oil

Glaze

1 egg yolk

2 tablespoons cold water

poppy seeds or sesame seeds (optional)

Makes 1 large loaf, 16 servings. Each serving: 87 calories; less than 1 gm dietary fiber; less than 1 gm soluble fiber; 15 gm carbohydrates; 3 gm protein; 2 gm fat (18% calories from fat); 34 mg cholesterol; 127 mg sodium; 22 mg potassium; 6 mg calcium.

Brioche

Never been to Paris? Having a brioche with your coffee is the next best thing. Light and subtly sweet, brioches are a treat you'll want to perfect. Mary likes to use a quarter of this recipe for doughnuts, a quarter for coffee cake, a quarter for Danish pastry, and a quarter for Beef Wellington. Bon appetit!

no stick cooking spray

1 package (5/16 ounce) HODGSON MILL ACTIVE DRY YEAST

1 cup skim milk, scalded and cooled to 115° F.

3 1/2 to 4 cups HODGSON MILL UNBLEACHED FLOUR

1 cup HODGSON MILL BEST FOR BREAD WHITE FLOUR

1/4 cup granulated sugar

1 teaspoon salt

1/2 cup soft margarine

3 eggs

2 egg whites, beaten

sugar for sprinkling (optional)

"As the dough goes into the oven, so the loaves come out." — *French Proverb*

Spray a large bowl with no stick cooking spray.

Blend yeast and warm milk and allow to rest for 5 minutes.

Blend 2 1/2 cups flour and 1 cup HODGSON MILL BEST FOR BREAD WHITE FLOUR with sugar and salt in a large bowl. Pour yeast mixture over flour mixture with margarine and eggs. Blend to make a smooth dough. Turn onto a floured board and knead to incorporate only enough of the remaining flour to make a smooth and elastic dough. Place in prepared bowl and cover with plastic wrap and a wet towel. Allow to rise in a warm, draft-free place until dough doubles in bulk, about 1 hour.

Prepare 24 brioche pans or muffin tins by spraying with no stick cooking spray. Divide dough into 24 balls. Divide the balls into 2 pieces, 1 large and 1 small. Put each large ball into prepared pan or muffin tin or on baking sheet. Flour your fingers, make an indentation in each large ball, and put the small ball in the indentation. Cover and allow dough to rise in a warm, draft-free place for 30 to 40 minutes, until almost doubled.

Preheat oven to 350° F. Brush rolls with the egg white and sprinkle with sugar. Bake 10 to 15 minutes, until rolls are golden brown.

Continued on next page

Brioche

Continued from previous page

Makes 24 brioches. Each brioche: 144 calories; less than 1 gm dietary fiber; less than 1 gm soluble fiber; 21 gm carbohydrates; 4 gm protein; 5 gm fat (30% calories from fat); 34 mg cholesterol; 151 mg sodium; 56 mg potassium; 22 mg calcium.

Variations:

To make rolls without brioche pans: After first rise, form dough into balls 3 to 4 inches in diameter. Put each ball on a prepared baking sheet. Cover, allow to rise in a warm, draft-free place. After the final rise, make an *X* in the top of each roll with kitchen scissors. Sprinkle with sugar. Bake at 350° F. for 10 to 15 minutes.

Glazed Doughnuts: On a floured board, roll dough to thickness of 1/4 inch. Cut into 3 inch rounds with a 1 inch doughnut hole. Cover and allow to rise in a warm, draft-free place for 1 hour. Heat vegetable oil in a large heavy pan or a deep fat fryer to 375° F. (at this temperature, a bread cube will brown quickly). Fry doughnuts and holes, a few at a time, 2 to 3 minutes per side. Make glaze by blending 1 cup confectioners sugar with 1 tablespoon milk and 1/2 teaspoon vanilla. Glaze warm doughnuts.

Brown Sugar Coffee Cake: Mix 3/4 cup walnuts, with 1 cup firmly packed brown sugar, 1 teaspoon cinnamon, and 1 cup raisins. Roll 1/4 brioche recipe into a rectangle 24 x 8 inches. Spread with nut mixture. Roll, jelly roll style, into a 24 x 2-inch tube. Form dough into a circle and put, seam side down, on a baking sheet that has been sprayed with no stick cooking spray. With scissors, make 12 slashes in

Continued on next page

Brioche

Continued from previous page

the dough. You can make a petal design by turning the flaps of dough alternately inward and outward. Cover and allow to rise in a warm, draft-free place for 1 hour. Preheat oven to 350° F. Brush dough with egg white and sprinkle with sugar. Bake for 35 minutes, until ring is nicely browned.

Danish Pastry: Simmer 1 cup dried apricots in just enough water to cover until tender, about 30 minutes. Drain, cut up, and mix with 1/3 cup sugar and 1/4 teaspoon allspice. Roll 1/4 brioche dough into a 16 inch square. Cut into 4 x 4 inch squares and place them 1/2 inch apart on an ungreased baking sheet. Top with a scant 2 teaspoons apricot filling (or jam). Bring 2 opposite corners to the center, pressing firmly to seal. Cover and allow to rise in a warm, draft-free place for 30 minutes. Preheat oven to 400° F. Bake until deep golden brown, about 20 minutes. If desired, glaze with confectioners frosting (see above Doughnut recipe).

Beef Wellington: Trim and clean fat from a 5 pound beef tenderloin. Roast in a 425° F. oven for 25 minutes or until very rare (meat temperature is 120° F.) Brown 1/2 pound finely chopped mushrooms and 1/2 cup shallots or green onions in 1/4 cup olive oil. Take 1/4 of brioche dough and cut into two pieces. Roll out one piece into a large rectangle, 1 1/2 inches longer and wider than the beef. Put on a baking sheet that has been sprayed with no stick cooking spray. Spread rectangle with mushroom mixture. Put meat on dough, leaving equal amount of uncovered dough on all sides. Roll out rest of dough and shape it over the meat. Secure top and bottom pieces together, pinching all around the meat. Brush with beaten egg white. Bake for 10 minutes, then reduce oven to 375° F. Bake until crust is golden, about 20 more minutes. Let stand for 15 minutes before slicing.

Baguettes

A slender, crusty version of French bread, a baguette loaf is best served immediately after baking. Day-old baguettes make delicious garlic rounds. If you want perfectly shaped loaves, use special baguette pans, available at cookware shops. Dust with flour before baking for a continental flair.

Spray a large bowl with no stick cooking spray.

Blend warm water with yeast and allow mixture to rest for 5 minutes. Add HODGSON MILL BEST FOR BREAD WHITE FLOUR, 1 1/2 cups unbleached flour, and salt. Mix to form a smooth dough. Turn onto a floured board and knead, adding flour to make dough smooth and satiny. This takes about 5 minutes.

Put dough into prepared bowl, cover with plastic wrap and a wet towel. Allow to rise in a warm, draft-free place for 1 hour. Dough will be almost doubled in bulk.

Knead dough down and divide into 2 balls. Cover and let rest for 10 minutes. Spray a baking sheet (or baguette pans) with no stick cooking spray.

Shape each ball into a 16 x 8 inch rectangle. Roll up tightly from long side. Seal well, tapering ends. Place on prepared baking sheet. Cover, and allow to rise in a warm, draft-free place for 1 hour. Dough will be nearly doubled in bulk.

Preheat oven to 375° F. Brush with water. With a sharp knife, make 3 or 4 diagonal cuts, about 1/4 inch deep, across the top of the loaves. Brush with egg white and sprinkle with poppy seeds, if desired. Bake for 30 minutes, until loaves are golden brown.

no stick coooking spray

1 package (5/16 ounce) HODGSON MILL ACTIVE DRY YEAST

1 1/4 cups warm water, 115° F.

1 cup HODGSON MILL BEST FOR BREAD WHITE FLOUR

2 cups HODGSON MILL UNBLEACHED FLOUR

1 teaspoon salt

1 egg white

poppy seeds (optional)

"It is better to pay the baker than the doctor."
— French Proverb

Continued on next page

Baguettes

Continued from previous page

Makes two, 16 inch long baguettes, about 8 servings each. Each serving: 80 calories; less than 1 gm dietary fiber; less than 1 gm soluble fiber; 17 gm carbohydrates; 3 gm protein; 1 gm fat (2% calories from fat); 0 mg cholesterol; 126 mg sodium; 27 mg potassium; 5 mg calcium.

Variation:

Garlic rounds: Preheat oven to broil. Heat 1/4 cup extra virgin olive oil. Add 3 cloves garlic, minced, and sauté until deep brown. Cut day-old baguette into 1/2 inch rounds and place on ungreased baking sheet. Brush with garlic-flavored olive oil. Brush onto one side of bread rounds. Top with finely grated Parmesan cheese and finely chopped fresh basil. Broil until cheese is melted and browned.

Focaccia

The crust of this pizza-like dish is a chewy hearth bread. It's wonderfully crisp because it's baked beforehand. Mary likes to top it with ripe tomatoes and fresh herbs, but other vegetables, lean ground beef, and chicken strips are good, too. Focaccia tastes best right out of the oven.

Pour 1 tablespoon olive oil into a large bowl. Set aside.

Blend yeast with the warm water, and gradually add 1 1/4 cups flour. Knead lightly until dough is smooth and elastic, about 5 minutes. Put in oiled bowl and turn to coat thoroughly. Cover and allow to stand in a warm, draft-free place until doubled in bulk, about 1 hour.

Knead down dough and add 1/4 cup warm water, 3 tablespoons olive oil, Parmesan cheese, remaining flour, basil, and salt. Mix well, then knead dough to a smooth, elastic consistency, adding more flour if necessary.

Preheat oven to 400° F. Spray 1 large or 2 small pizza pans with no stick cooking spray. Roll dough to fit pan. Brush with remaining olive oil. Bake for 20 to 25 minutes until the Focaccia is brown and crisp.

Meanwhile, place tomatos, olive oil, garlic, and basil in a blender cup. Pulse several times to make a chunky sauce. Salt and pepper to taste. Spoon onto Focaccia crust, top with cheese, and bake until cheese melts, about 5 minutes.

Makes 8 servings. Each serving: 332 calories; 2 gm dietary fiber; 1 gm soluble fiber; 36 gm carbohydrates; 8 gm protein; 18 gm fat (48% calories from fat); 5 mg cholesterol; 365 mg sodium; 155 mg potassium; 99 mg calcium.

6 tablespoons extra virgin olive oil

1 package (5/16 ounce) HODGSON MILL ACTIVE DRY YEAST

1/2 cup warm water, 115° F.

2 1/2 to 3 cups HODGSON MILL UNBLEACHED FLOUR

1/4 cup warm water

1/2 cup freshly grated Parmesan cheese

1/4 cup fresh basil, coarsely chopped*

1 teaspoon salt

3 large tomatoes

3 tablespoons olive oil

2 cloves garlic, sliced

1/2 cup fresh basil leaves*

salt to taste

freshly ground pepper

1/4 cup freshly grated Parmesan cheese

* If fresh basil is not available, use fresh Italian parsley. If you use dry basil, use 1/3 less.

Sourdough Starter

Popular with early settlers, because it kept well and could be made easily in a trailside camp, Sourdough Bread is being rediscovered in California and Alaska.

The Sourdough Starter is a kind of leavening, which keeps for five days at room temperature, and for 10 days in the refrigerator. Ingredients are added to the starter to make sourdough bread. The starter is replenished each time it's used.

The following recipe for starter is accompanied by recipes for several sourdough breads. Mary likes to make a batch of Sourdough Starter and use part of it for Sourdough Cinnamon Bread, part for Buckwheat Pancakes, and part for Friendship Cake or Health Bread.

1 package (5/16 ounce) HODGSON MILL ACTIVE DRY YEAST

2 cups warm water, 115° F.

2 cups HODGSON MILL UNBLEACHED FLOUR

Combine yeast, water, and flour in a large, glass mixing bowl. Stir until the mixture is smooth. Cover the container with a cheese cloth or other cloth and allow to stand at room temperature for at least 2 days. Stir several times each day.

The starter is ready to use when it is bubbly and has a slightly acidic odor. After removing the starter you need for a particular sourdough recipe, replenish the remainder by adding 1 cup of flour and 1 cup warm water.

Stir several times a day. The starter may be refrigerated after it becomes bubbly. Simply cover and refrigerate. If you don't use it for 10 days, stir in 1/2 teaspoon sugar. If you store the starter in a jar at room temperature, cover it with a light cloth. Never seal the jar tightly when the starter is at room temperature.

"Without a bit of bread even a palace is sad; with it, a pine tree is a palace."
— *Russian Proverb*

Sourdough Bread

Don't be put off by the name. Basic sourdough is a hearty bread, chewy, with a little tang, a coarse crumb, and a lot of flavor. Try all the Sourdough Bread variations, and your fans will cheer you on!

In large glass bowl, combine warm water with Sourdough Starter, 3 cups unbleached flour, HODGSON MILL BEST FOR BREAD WHITE FLOUR, sugar, and salt. Mix thoroughly, then cover with a damp cheese cloth and allow to rise in a warm, draft-free place for 6 to 8 hours, or until doubled in bulk.

Blend baking soda with remaining 1 1/2 cups of flour. On a floured board, knead the remaining flour into dough until it's smooth and satiny. This takes 10 to 15 minutes.

Spray a baking sheet with no stick cooking spray. Divide dough in half and shape each half into a ball or a long loaf. Cover with a damp cloth and allow to rise in a warm, draft-free place for 2 to 3 hours, until loaves have almost doubled in size.

Preheat oven to 400° F. Brush loaves with water, slash them with a sharp knife, and sprinkle with a little white flour, if desired. Bake 30 to 40 minutes, or until crust is golden brown.

Makes 2 loaves, 12 slices each loaf. Each slice: 284 calories; 2 gm dietary fiber; 1 gm soluble fiber; 60 gm carbohydrates; 8 gm protein; less than 1 gm fat (2% calories from fat) ; no cholesterol; 314 mg sodium; 78 mg potassium; 14 mg calcium.

1 1/2 cups warm water

1 cup Sourdough Starter, room temperature (page 96)

4 1/2 to 5 cups HODGSON MILL UNBLEACHED FLOUR

1 cup HODGSON MILL BEST FOR BREAD WHITE FLOUR

3 teaspoons sugar

1 1/2 teaspoons salt

1 teaspoon baking soda

no stick cooking spray

"A bag full of flour and a purse full of money are the best relations in the world."
— *Roumanian Proverb*

Sourdough Cinnamon Bread

Unlike a traditional sourdough bread, this one has a light crumb. It makes marvelous toast, especially if you add raisins to the cinnamon sugar as indicated.

no stick cooking spray

2 cups HODGSON MILL UNBLEACHED FLOUR

1 cup HODGSON MILL BEST FOR BREAD WHITE FLOUR

1 teaspoon HODGSON MILL ACTIVE DRY YEAST

1/2 teaspoon salt

1 cup Sourdough Starter, room temperature (page 96)

1/2 cup buttermilk

1/4 cup melted margarine

1 teaspoon cinnamon

1/3 cup sugar

1/2 cup raisins (optional)

"The bread at home is always good."
— Italian Proverb

Spray a large bowl with no stick cooking spray.

Combine 1 1/2 cups unbleached flour with HODGSON MILL BEST FOR BREAD WHITE FLOUR, yeast, and salt. Stir to blend evenly. Add Sourdough Starter and buttermilk, then mix by hand or in an electric mixer or in a food processor fitted with a dough hook. Turn onto floured board, and add enough flour to make a slightly sticky dough. Continue to knead until dough is smooth and satiny.

Place dough in prepared bowl. Cover with plastic wrap and a wet towel. Allow to rise in a warm, draft-free place for 1 hour until dough doubles in bulk.

Meanwhile, blend margarine with cinnamon, sugar, and raisins. Spray a 9 x 5 x 3-inch bread pan with no stick cooking spray.

Knead dough down, then place on a floured board. With a rolling pin, roll into a large rectangular sheet, 18 x 8 inches long. Spread cinnamon mixture over the entire rectangle. Roll up tightly to make a cylinder of bread 8 inches long.

Put bread in prepared bread pan. Cover and allow to rise in a warm, draft-free place for 1 1/2 to 2 hours. Bread will rise over top of pan. Preheat oven to 350° F. Bake for 30 minutes, or until bread is golden brown. Allow to cool completely before slicing.

Makes 1 loaf, 12 servings. Each serving: 252 calories; 2 gm dietary fiber; 1 gm soluble fiber; 48 gm carbohydrates; 6 gm protein; 4 gm fat (15% calories from fat); less than 1 mg cholesterol; 143 mg sodium; 120 mg potassium; 27 mg calcium.

Sourdough
Health Bread

This bread's rye flavor and dense crumb make it the perfect loaf for toast and sandwiches.

Spray a large bowl with no stick cooking spray.

Stir together 1 1/2 cups 50/50 flour, rye flour, HODGSON MILL BEST FOR BREAD WHITE FLOUR, soda, and salt. Combine buttermilk, Sourdough Starter, honey, and vegetable oil.

With an electric mixer or by hand, stir wet ingredients into dry ingredients, blending well. Turn onto a floured board and knead in remaining flour. Knead until dough is well blended and firm, about 5 minutes.

Put in prepared bowl. Cover with plastic wrap and a wet towel. Allow to rise in a warm, draft-free place for 1 hour, until dough is almost doubled.

Spray a 9 x 5 x 3-inch bread pan with no stick cooking spray. Preheat oven to 325° F. Knead down dough. Form into a loaf and put in prepared pan. Bake for 1 hour. Cool completely before slicing.

Makes 1 loaf, 10 servings. Each serving: 227 calories; 3 gm dietary fiber; less than 1 gm soluble fiber; 69 gm carbohydrates; 11 gm protein; 4 gm fat (10% calories from fat) ; less than 1 mg cholesterol; 289 mg sodium; 129 mg potassium; 41 mg calcium.

no stick cooking spray

2 cups HODGSON MILL 50/50 FLOUR

1/2 cup HODGSON MILL RYE FLOUR

1/2 cup HODGSON MILL BEST FOR BREAD WHITE FLOUR

2 teaspoons baking soda

1/2 teaspoon salt

1 cup buttermilk, lukewarm

1 cup Sourdough Starter, room temperature (page 96)

2 tablespoons honey

2 tablespoons vegetable oil

"It is necessary to eat several loaves together before knowing anyone."
— *Italian Proverb*

Sourdough Buckwheat Pancakes

This pancake is light and delicious. Mary makes the recipe the night before serving. Then, at breakfast she adds 1/2 cup warm water to the batter, and the pancakes are ready to pour!

1 cup HODGSON MILL BUCKWHEAT FLOUR

1 teaspoon baking powder

1 teaspoon sugar

1/8 teaspoon salt

1 egg

1 cup Sourdough Starter, room temperature (page 96)

1/2 cup buttermilk, lukewarm

no stick cooking spray

Combine flour, baking powder, sugar, and salt. Lightly beat egg and add to starter. Add buttermilk. Stir wet ingredients into dry ingredients and blend until smooth.

Spray a griddle or a large fry pan with no stick cooking spray. Heat griddle to medium hot. Pour pancakes, 1/3 cup at a time, onto griddle. Flip pancakes when bubbles start to form on top side.

Makes 4 servings of 3 pancakes each. Each serving: 335 calories; 2 gm dietary fiber; 1 gm soluble fiber; 67 gm carbohydrates; 10 gm protein; 3 gm fat (7% calories from fat) ; 70 mg cholesterol; 194 mg sodium; 214 mg potassium; 70 mg calcium.

"Words do not make flour."
— *Italian Proverb*

Sourdough Friendship Cake

One Valentine's Day, several years ago, Mary sent one of these Friendship Cakes to each of four local television stations. Not only did she make friends, she was also booked for spots on three talk shows! The combination of cinnamon, apples, nuts, and chocolate is irresistible. Serve with coffee some afternoon, and you will be, too.

Prepare a large bundt pan by spraying with no stick cooking spray. Preheat oven to 350° F.

Gently combine Sourdough Starter with oil, vanilla, and eggs. Blend flour, sugar, baking powder, salt, cinnamon, and baking soda. Fold wet ingredients into dry ingredients. Fold in apples, chocolate morsels, walnuts, and coconut.

Pour into prepared pan. Bake for 40 to 50 minutes. Cake is baked when it pulls away from the sides of the pan. Allow cake to cool for 10 minutes before removing from pan.

Makes 16 servings. Each serving: 336 calories; 2 gm dietary fiber; less than 1 gm soluble fiber; 44 gm carbohydrates; 5 gm protein; 16 gm fat (42% calories from fat) ; 51 mg cholesterol; 195 mg sodium; 121 mg potassium; 26 mg calcium.

no stick cooking spray

1 1/2 cups Sourdough Starter (page 96)

2/3 cup vegetable oil (or 1/2 cup oil and 1/3 cup brandy)

3 eggs

2 teaspoons vanilla

2 cups HODGSON MILL UNBLEACHED FLOUR

1 cup sugar

2 teaspoons baking powder

1/2 teaspoon salt

1 1/2 teaspoons cinnamon

1 1/2 teaspoons baking soda

2 apples, cored and chopped

1 cup chocolate morsels

1/2 cup chopped walnuts

1/2 cup coconut

Traditional Italian Bread

This delicious crusty bread is simplicity itself; it's hearty and has plenty of character. Mary says the secret is using bread flour with the traditional blend of whole wheat and white flours. Italian Bread dough also makes great pizza crust.

no stick cooking spray

1 package (5/16 ounce) **HODGSON MILL ACTIVE DRY YEAST**

4 cups warm water, 115° F.

2 teaspoons salt

6 1/2 to 7 cups **HODGSON MILL 50/50 FLOUR**

1 cup **HODGSON MILL BEST FOR BREAD WHITE FLOUR**

"My house, my wife, bread and garlic; my life."
— Italian Proverb

Spray a large bowl with no stick cooking spray.

In a small bowl, blend yeast with 1 cup warm water and allow to rest for 5 minutes. Place 3 cups water with salt in a second large bowl. Add the yeast. Blend 5 cups 50/50 flour with HODGSON MILL BEST FOR BREAD WHITE FLOUR. Pour flour into water, stirring as you pour. When dough is stiff, turn onto a floured board and knead it into a smooth, elastic ball, adding flour if necessary. This takes about 10 minutes.

Put dough in prepared bowl and turn to coat thoroughly. Cover with plastic wrap, then with a damp towel, and allow to rise in a warm, draft-free place for about 1 hour. The dough will almost double in bulk.

Spray a baking sheet with no stick cooking spray. Turn the dough onto a floured board and knead down. Cut the dough into 4 pieces and form into 4 loaves, 12 inches long and 3 inches wide.

Put on prepared sheet, cover with plastic wrap, and allow to rise in a warm, draft-free place for 1 hour. Preheat oven to 425° F. Bake bread 35 to 45 minutes. During the first few minutes of baking, throw 3 to 4 ice cubes onto the oven floor to create steam. This will make a crisp crust. Remove the bread from the sheet and reduce oven temperature to 350° F. Put bread back in the oven directly on oven rack to finish baking. Bake until golden brown, about 20 more minutes.

Makes 4 loaves, 6 servings each loaf. Each serving: 137 calories; 3 gm dietary fiber; less than 1 gm soluble fiber; 29 gm carbohydrates; 5 gm protein; less than 1 gm fat (3% calories from fat); 0 mg cholesterol; 164 mg sodium; 88 mg potassium; 11 mg calcium.

Flour Tortillas

Tortillas are the cornerstone of the Mexican diet. These tortillas are the traditional size and texture.

In a large mixing bowl, blend the white flour, salt, and baking powder. Stir in warm water until mixture is blended and sticks together.

Form into 12 balls and put between 2 pieces of waxed paper. With a tortilla press or a rolling pin, flatten each ball into a circle 5 to 6 inches in diameter. Spray a griddle or a large frying pan with no stick cooking spray and heat. Bake each tortilla 1 1/2 to 2 minutes per side. Tortilla will be speckled and brown when cooked.

Makes 12 tortillas. Each tortilla: 88 calories; less than 1 gm dietary fiber; less than 1 gm soluble fiber; 18 gm carbohydrates; 3 gm protein; less than 1 gm fat (2% calories from fat) 0 mg cholesterol; 192 mg sodium; 23 mg potassium; 10 mg calcium.

Variations

Oat Bran Tortillas: Substitute 1 cup HODGSON MILL OAT BRAN HOT CEREAL for 1 cup unbleached flour.
Whole Wheat Tortillas: Substitute HODGSON MILL 50/50 FLOUR for unbleached flour.

2 1/2 cups HODGSON MILL UNBLEACHED FLOUR
1 teaspoon salt
1 teaspoon baking powder
1 to 1 1/4 cups warm water
no stick cooking spray

"Peace and bread to you."
— Spanish Proverb

Corn Tortillas

Corn meal gives these tortillas an authentic Southwestern flavor. They are a delicious way to begin lots of great Mexican meals and make terrific taco chips, too.

1 cup HODGSON MILL WHITE OR YELLOW CORN MEAL

1 cup HODGSON MILL UNBLEACHED FLOUR

1 teaspoon salt

1 teaspoon baking soda

3/4 cup warm water

no stick cooking spray

In a large mixing bowl, blend the corn meal the white flour, salt, and baking powder. Stir in warm water until mixture is blended and sticks together.

Form into 12 balls. Place the balls between 2 pieces of waxed paper. With a tortilla press or a rolling pin, flatten each ball into a circle 5 to 6 inches in diameter. Spray a griddle or a large frying pan with no stick cooking spray and heat. Bake each tortilla 1 1/2 to 2 minutes per side. Tortilla will be speckled and brown when cooked.

Makes 12 tortillas.   Each tortilla: 77 calories; less than 1 gm dietary fiber; less than 1 gm soluble fiber; 16 gm carbohydrates; 2 gm protein; less than 1 gm fat (3% calories from fat); 0 mg cholesterol; 232 mg sodium; 23 mg potassium; 3 mg calcium.

Lebanese Pita Bread

Pita bread, also called Syrian, Armenian, Middle Eastern bread, and pocket bread, can be served in hundreds of delicious ways. It's very good just toasted and buttered. Stuffed with cheese, marinated vegetables, or chopped meat, it also makes wonderful portable sandwiches. This recipe calls for oat bran hot cereal, but feel free to experiment with whole wheat flour, rye flour, or unbleached flour.

In a food processor fitted with a steel blade or in a blender, mill the oat bran hot cereal until fine and flour-like, about 2 minutes. Blend the oat bran hot cereal with the yeast and 1/2 cup of the flour. Combine the warm water, oil, and salt. Pour over the flour-yeast mixture.

Spray a medium-sized bowl with no stick cooking spray.

Beat at low speed in an electric mixer fitted a with dough hook or in a food processor for 1 minute, scraping sides of bowl. Beat for 3 minutes at medium speed to incorporate as much of the remaining flour as possible.

Turn onto a floured board and knead in enough of the remaining flour to make a smooth, satiny dough. This takes 5 to 7 minutes. Put dough in prepared bowl, cover, and allow it to rise in a warm, draft-free place for 30 minutes. Dough should be very warm and light to touch. Knead down and divide into 12 equal portions. Cover, and allow dough to rise in a warm, draft-free place for 15 minutes.

Preheat oven to 500 ° F. To roll out pitas: cut 12 pieces of plastic wrap or waxed paper. Place one side of the paper on the bottom surface of a 6 inch tortilla press or a flat plate. Place pita dough on paper, then fold paper over it. Use tortilla press, a flat plate, or a rolling pin to flatten dough to form a smooth, 1/8 inch thick pitas. Make sure the pitas have no creases or folds.

Continued on next page

1 1/2 cups HODGSON MILL OAT BRAN HOT CEREAL

1 package (5/16 ounce) HODGSON MILL ACTIVE DRY YEAST

2 to 2 1/2 cups HODGSON MILL UNBLEACHED FLOUR (divided)

1 1/4 cups very warm water, 115° F.

1/4 cup vegetable oil

1 1/2 teaspoons salt

no stick cooking spray

"Give bread for bread and do not let your neighbor go hungry."
— *Algerian Proverb*

Lebanese Pita Bread

Continued from previous page

Place the pitas, 4 at a time, on oven racks. The pitas should be distributed evenly around the oven. Bake for 3 minutes to set the dough. Then, turn pitas over and bake for 2 to 3 minutes more. The pitas brown and puff up as they bake.* Allow the oven to reheat for 5 minutes between baking periods.

To serve, open pitas to form pockets. Stuff pocket with meats, sautéed vegetables, or other fillings. If the pocket does not open easily, slit with a sharp knife.

* To ensure that pitas puff up, the dough must be warm, the pitas must be distributed evenly throughout the oven, and the oven must be *very* hot.

Makes 12 pitas. Each pita: 170 calories; 2 gm dietary fiber; 1 gm soluble fiber; 25 gm carbohydrates; 3 gm protein; 5 gm fat (30% calories from fat); 0 mg cholesterol; 245 mg sodium; 32 mg potassium; 6 mg calcium.

Water Bagels

Bagels are crisp and smooth on the outside and soft and moist inside. They take some time and skill to make, but are well worth it. You'll be glad to know that these water bagels are very low in fat. Spread with cream cheese, topped with lox and onion, or just toasted and buttered, bagels make a satisfying snack.

Spray a large cookie sheet with a thick coating of no stick cooking spray.

Blend 2 cups flour with yeast. Combine warm water, sugar, cinnamon, and salt and pour over the flour mixture.

Beat with an electric mixer or with a food processor fitted with dough hook for 1/2 minute. Blend in remaining flour and knead with mixer or food processor (or by hand) until the dough is smooth and satiny, 10 minutes by hand, or 4 minutes in an electric mixer or a food processor fitted with a dough hook.

Cover dough and allow it to rise in a warm, draft-free place for 30 minutes. Divide into 12 portions and shape each one into a smooth ball. Make a 1 inch hole in the center of each ball and shape dough into a 4 inch bagel. Put bagel on prepared cookie sheet. Cover; allow to rise in a warm, draft-free place for 20 minutes. Preheat oven to broil.

Broil the bagels for 5 minutes, 5 inches from the source of heat. Turn the bagels one time, but do not allow them to brown.

Reduce oven temperature to 375 ° F. On top of the stove, heat 1 gallon of water to boiling. Cook the bagels in boiling water, 4 to 5 at a time, for 7 minutes, turning once. Drain.
Put hot bagels on a greased baking sheet. Bake in a 375 ° F. oven

Continued on next page

no stick cooking spray

1 package (5/16 ounce) HODGSON MILL ACTIVE DRY YEAST

3 1/2 to 4 cups HODGSON MILL UNBLEACHED FLOUR (divided)

1 1/2 cups very warm water, 115° F.

3 tablespoons granulated sugar

1/2 teaspoon cinnamon

1 teaspoon salt

Water Bagels

Continued from previous page

Put hot bagels on a greased baking sheet. Bake in a 375° F. oven 25 to 30 minutes. When done, bagels will be deep brown, with a crisp outer crust.

Freeze any bagels not eaten in 2 days. To reheat, defrost, split, and toast in an electric toaster.

Makes 12 bagels. Each bagel: 153 calories; 1 gm dietary fiber; less than 1 gm soluble fiber; 33 gm carbohydrates; 4 gm protein; less than 1 gm fat (2% calories from fat) ; 0 mg cholesterol; 164 mg sodium; 46 mg potassium; 9 mg calcium.

Continued on next page

Water Bagels

Continued from previous page

Variations

Raisin Bagels: Add 1/2 cup raisins with the second flour addition.

Onion Bagels: Add 1/2 cup minced, sautéed onions with second flour addition.

Sesame Bagels.: Add 1/3 cup toasted sesame seeds with second flour addition. Before baking, brush bagels with milk and sprinkle with more sesame seeds.

Poppy Seed Bagels: Add 1/4 cup poppy seeds with second flour addition. Before baking, brush bagels with milk and sprinkle with more poppy seeds.

Rye-caraway Bagels: Substitute 1 1/2 cups HODGSON MILL RYE FLOUR for the unbleached flour. Add 1/4 cup caraway seeds with second flour addition.

Oat Bran Bagels: In a blender cup, mill 1 cup HODGSON MILL OAT BRAN HOT CEREAL until fine and flour-like. Substitute for 1 cup unbleached flour.

Whole Wheat Bagels: Substitute HODGSON MILL 50/50 FLOUR for unbleached flour.

Scotch Scones

Mary has adapted this highland delicacy to today's health conscious diet. It's fiber-rich, bursting with flavor, and delightfully soft and flaky. Spread with preserves or marmalade, take a bite, and you'll be in heaven.

3 cups HODGSON MILL OAT BRAN HOT CEREAL

1/2 cup currants

2 tablespoons granulated sugar

3 teaspoons baking powder

1/2 teaspoon salt

1/2 teaspoon soda

1/2 cup lowfat yogurt

1/4 cup peanut oil

2 large egg whites

2 tablespoons lowfat milk for brushing tops of scones

2 tablespoons granulated sugar for sprinkling tops of scones

Preheat oven to 400 ° F.

In a food processor fitted with a steel blade or in a blender, mill the oat bran hot cereal until fine and flour-like, about 2 minutes.

In a large bowl, combine the finely milled oat bran hot cereal with currants, sugar, baking powder, salt, soda, yogurt, peanut oil, and egg whites. Blend until the mixture holds together well.

Put mixture on a pastry board that has been sprinkled lightly with oat bran hot cereal. Knead dough lightly, about 1 minute. Divide into 12 portions. Flatten and form into 2 inch circles then flatten them to 1 inch thick. Brush tops with milk and sprinkle with sugar.

Place the scones, 2 inches apart, on an ungreased cookie sheet. Bake 10 to 12 minutes, or until the scones are golden brown. Serve hot.

Makes 12 scones. Each scone: 147 calories; 3 gm dietary fiber; 2 gm soluble fiber; 19 gm carbohydrates; 3 gm protein; 6 gm fat (40% calories from fat) ; less than 1 mg cholesterol; 217 mg sodium; 35 mg potassium; 36 mg calcium.

Hot Cross Buns

It's good luck to eat Hot Cross Buns on Good Friday, but they taste so wonderful, you'll want to make them every week! Sweet and spicy, packed with currants, these buns are just the thing with a hot cup of herbal tea.

In a mixing bowl or a food processor, blend 2 1/2 cups flour, yeast, sugar, salt, nutmeg, and cinnamon. Heat buttermilk to almost boiling, add margarine, and stir until melted. Pour buttermilk mixture into flour mixture, and blend with wooden spoon or dough hook. Add egg and currants. Knead in enough of the remaining flour to make a smooth, satiny dough, about 10 minutes by hand or 5 minutes with mixer or food processor.

Spray a medium-sized bowl with no stick cooking spray. Put dough in bowl, cover, and allow to rise in a warm, draft-free place for 20 minutes. Spray a 10 x 10 inch square baking pan with no stick cooking spray. Put dough on cutting board and cut into 16 parts. Form into 16 smooth balls and put in baking pan. Cover, and allow to rise in a warm, draft-free place for 15 minutes. Brush tops with egg white. Preheat oven to 425° F. Bake for 12 to 15 minutes until Hot Cross Buns are evenly browned. Let buns cool in pan.

To make icing, blend confectioners sugar and hot milk into a smooth paste. With icing, make a cross on top of each cooled bun.

Makes 16 buns. Each Hot Cross Bun: 124 calories; 2 gm dietary fiber; less than 1 gm soluble fiber; 24 gm carbohydrates; 4 gm protein; 1 gm fat (11% calories from fat); 18 gm cholesterol; 129 gm sodium; 99 gm potassium; 29 mg calcium.

3 cups HODGSON MILL 50/50 FLOUR

1 package (5/16 ounce) HODGSON MILL ACTIVE DRY YEAST

1/4 cup sugar

3/4 teaspoon salt

1/4 teaspoon nutmeg

1/4 teaspoon cinnamon

1 cup buttermilk

2 tablespoons light margarine

1 egg, beaten

1/3 cup currants

1 egg white, beaten

1 cup confectioners sugar

2 teaspoons hot milk

no stick cooking spray

"Bread of your own earning tastes sweet."
— *English Proverb*

Russian Blini

Try this Russian treat for breakfast. Made with buckwheat flour, it's like a heavy crepe or a raised pancake. Blini are low in calories and high in fiber. They are delicious topped with yogurt, fruit, or cottage cheese.

1 package (5/16 ounce) HODGSON MILL ACTIVE DRY YEAST

1/2 cup very warm water

1 cup plain lowfat yogurt, room temperature

1 teaspoon granulated sugar

1/2 teaspoon salt

1 tablespoon peanut oil

1 cup HODGSON MILL BUCKWHEAT FLOUR

1 cup warm water

2 large egg whites

no stick cooking spray

Sprinkle yeast over hot water. Stir and allow the mixture to cure for 5 minutes until yeast is bubbly. Blend yogurt with sugar, salt, and oil. Stir the yeast mixture into this mixture. Add buckwheat and beat by hand or with an electric mixer until batter is smooth.

Cover the bowl and allow to stand in a warm, draft-free place for 20 minutes. Meanwhile, whip egg whites until soft peaks form. Fold the last cup of warm water into the batter, then fold egg whites into the batter and let stand for another 10 minutes.*

Preheat the oven to 250 ° F. Spray a Blini pan or a 6 inch crepe pan with no stick cooking spray. Heat the pan over a medium hot burner (if you are using an electric pan, heat to 375° F.). Place a scant 1/4 cup batter in the pan and cook until top is firm and bubbly. Turn blini and cook until crisp and golden brown, about 5 minutes. Warm in the oven until ready to serve. Repeat to make 12 Blini.

You may store Blini, covered, in the refrigerator for up to 3 weeks or wrap and freeze them for up to 3 months. To reheat, microwave each Blini for 20 seconds (high), or heat in a 350° F. oven for 5 minutes.

Makes 12 blini. Each blini: 55 calories; less than 1 gm dietary fiber; less than 1 gm soluble fiber; 8 gm carbohydrates; 2 gm protein; 1.5 gm fat (24% calories from fat); 1 mg cholesterol; 103 mg sodium; 87 mg potassium; 37 mg calcium.

*To prepare the night before, make Blini recipe, excluding the final cup of warm water and the egg whites. Cover and refrigerate. In the morning, remove and add warm water. Whip eggs until soft peaks form, fold into batter, and continue as above.

"A house may be fine, but without bread it is miserable." — Russian Proverb

Dark
Pumpernickel Bread

The secret to a rich, dark pumpernickel is unsweetened cocoa. This is an authentic, hearty German bread, delicious with soups or in salami and cheese sandwiches.

In a medium saucepan, heat corn meal with water. Cook, stirring until thick and smooth, about 5 minutes. Remove from heat and add margarine, salt, sugar, caraway, cocoa, and molasses. Blend well.

Spray a large bowl with no stick cooking spray.

Pour corn meal mixture in second large bowl. Cool to 115° F. and add mashed potatoes and yeast. Blend in rye and whole wheat flours and HODGSON MILL BEST FOR BREAD WHITE FLOUR, kneading as you incorporate flour. Turn onto a floured board and continue kneading until dough is smooth and elastic, about 10 minutes.

Put in prepared bowl, turning to coat all sides of dough. Cover with plastic wrap and a wet towel. Allow to rise in a warm, draft-free place for 1 hour, or until dough has almost doubled.

Sprinkle a baking sheet with corn meal. Form into a ball or into a free form loaf and put on baking sheet. Cover and allow to rise in a warm, draft-free place for 1 hour. Bread will be almost double in bulk.

Preheat oven to 375° F. Brush loaf with egg white. Bake for 50 minutes, or until bread sounds hollow when tapped.

Makes 1 loaf, 16 servings. Each serving: 146 calories; 4 gm dietary fiber; less than 1 gm soluble fiber; 30 gm carbohydrates; 4 gm protein; 2 gm fat (9% calories from fat); 1 mg cholesterol; 220 mg sodium; 153 mg potassium; 35 mg calcium.

1/2 cup HODGSON MILL WHITE OR YELLOW CORN MEAL

1 3/4 cups water

1 tablespoon soft margarine

1 teaspoon salt

1 tablespoon sugar

2 tablespoons caraway seeds

1/4 cup unsweetened cocoa

3/4 cup dark molasses

no stick cooking spray

1 cup freshly mashed potatoes, made with skimmed milk

1 package (5/16 ounce) HODGSON MILL ACTIVE DRY YEAST

2 1/2 cups HODGSON MILL RYE FLOUR

1 cup HODGSON MILL WHOLE WHEAT GRAHAM FLOUR

1/2 cup HODGSON MILL BEST FOR BREAD WHITE FLOUR

white or yellow corn meal for baking sheet

1 egg white, beaten

HISTORICAL BREAD TALE

During the Middle Ages, townspeople made their own dough, but took it to neighborhood bake shops for baking. Bakers were notorious for pinching off a bit of dough from each loaf and using it for their own bread. Although this was against the law, it was overlooked as long as the amount of dough pinched was small. Greedy bakers were punished according to local custom.

In Hamburg, bakers with numerous offenses were sentenced to the "baker's gallows." The guilty baker was forced into a large basket suspended high above a huge mud puddle. This attracted crowds of townspeople who jeered and laughed at the baker swinging in the basket. His only alternative was to jump directly into the mud puddle and run home soaking wet and covered with mud.

Recipes for bread featured on the previous page are:
Calzone, Page 117
Pot Stickers, Page 124

CHAPTER 7

STUFFED BREADS
by Mary Ward

These hearty breads make marvelous lunches or dinners.
The variety of dishes you can make with unbleached and
whole grain flour is amazing.
Recipes include:

SPINACH STUFFED RYE ROUND

CALZONE

VEGETABLE TURNOVERS WITH SPINACH CHEESE FILLING

CARIBBEAN MEAT PATÉ

MINI TURKEY BURGERS

SPRING ROLLS

MUFFULETTA

POT STICKERS

BASIC PIZZA RECIPE

PIZZA PRIMAVERA

TRIPLE DECKER PIZZA

PEPPERONI BREAD

REUBEN ROLLS

CORNISH PASTIES

BULGUR BUNS WITH ALL-VEGETABLE STUFFING

Spinach Stuffed Rye Round

A spectacular appetizer that your guests will love. The zesty sour cream, spinach, and water chestnut filling complements the caraway rye shell perfectly. It can be prepared in advance and refrigerated. Just before serving, garnish with a sprig of fresh parsley, basil, or mint.

Filling

1 pound fresh spinach, cleaned

1 cup sour cream

1/2 cup mayonnaise

1/2 cup sliced water chestnuts

2 tablespoons minced onion

1 clove garlic, minced

1 teaspoon dill seed

2 tablespoons chopped pimento

salt to taste

freshly ground pepper

Bread Dough

no stick cooking spray

1 1/2 cups HODGSON MILL UNBLEACHED FLOUR

1/2 cup HODGSON MILL BEST FOR BREAD WHITE FLOUR

1 1/2 cups HODGSON MILL RYE FLOUR

1/2 teaspoon salt

1 package (5/16 ounce) HODGSON MILL ACTIVE DRY YEAST

2 tablespoons vegetable oil

1 tablespoon caraway seed

1 1/4 cups very warm water, 115° F.

Cook spinach and drain, pressing out all water. Chop coarsely. Blend with sour cream, mayonnaise, water chestnuts, onion, garlic, dill, and pimento. Salt and pepper to taste. Cover and refrigerate for at least 8 hours.

Spray a large bowl with no stick cooking spray.

In a another large mixing bowl, blend 1 cup unbleached flour with the HODGSON MILL BEST FOR BREAD WHITE FLOUR, rye flour, salt, and yeast. Stir thoroughly with a wooden spoon. Add the oil, caraway seed, and very warm water. Continue to stir until all ingredients are well blended. The dough will be stiff. Turn onto a floured board and knead in enough flour to make dough smooth and satiny. This will take about about 10 minutes. (This dough may also be mixed and kneaded in a food processor or mixer with a dough hook.)

Put dough in prepared bowl, turning to coat thoroughly. Cover with plastic wrap, and allow to rise in a warm, draft-free place for 1 hour. The dough will be warm, light, and almost doubled in bulk.

Spray a large cookie sheet with no stick cooking spray.

Knead down dough. Form an 8 inch round ball and put on prepared baking sheet. Cover and place in a warm, draft-free place for 1 hour. Preheat oven to 375° F. Bake for 45 minutes, or until rye bread is well browned and sounds hollow when tapped.

When loaf has cooled, hollow it out and fill with spinach dip. Tear bread into bite-sized portions, and use as dippers with spinach dip.

Makes 10 appetizer servings. Each serving: 264 calories; 2 gm dietary fiber; less than 1 gm soluble fiber; 35 gm carbohydrates; 7 gm protein; 11 gm fat (38% calories from fat); 14 mg cholesterol; 147 mg sodium; 337 mg potassium; 82 mg calcium.

Calzone

An extraordinary calzone that Mary enjoyed at a picturesque Italian restaurant in Heidelburg, Germany was the inspiration for this recipe. Mary's Calzone is filled with chives, garlic, and prosciutto, plus mozzarella and Parmesan cheese. It's been a favorite in the Ward home for many years. Mouthwatering!

Combine warm water and sugar with yeast in a medium-sized mixing bowl. Allow yeast to soften for 5 minutes. Add 1 1/2 cups flour, and knead until smooth. Add oil and salt, and gradually blend in remaining flour to make a firm dough. Turn out onto a lightly floured board and knead until smooth and satiny.

Spray a large bowl with no stick cooking spray. Put dough in bowl, turning to coat thoroughly. Cover with plastic wrap, then a damp towel. Allow to rise in a warm, draft-free place for about 1 hour, until dough is almost doubled.

Spray a large baking sheet with no stick cooking spray.

Knead down dough and divide into 3 pieces. On a lightly floured surface, roll each piece into a 9 inch circle. Place 1/3 mozzarella cheese, 1/3 Parmesan cheese, and 1/3 prosciutto on each circle of dough. Top with chives and garlic. Moisten edges and fold over to enclose the filling, pressing edges firmly together.

Place on baking sheet, cover lightly with plastic wrap, and allow to rise in a warm, draft-free place until dough feels light, about 35 minutes.

Preheat oven to 375° F. Bake for 30 to 35 minutes, or until Calzone is browned. Remove from oven and brush with oil. Sprinkle with grated Parmesan cheese. Serve warm with pizza sauce, if desired.

1 cup warm water

1/2 teaspoon sugar

1 package (5/16 ounce) HODGSON MILL ACTIVE DRY YEAST

3 cups HODGSON MILL 50/50 FLOUR

2 tablespoons vegetable oil

1/2 teaspoon salt

no stick cooking spray

12 ounces mozzarella cheese, shredded

2 ounces finely grated Parmesan cheese

3 ounces sliced prosciutto, cut into strips

3 tablespoons chopped chives

1 tablespoon minced garlic

1 tablespoon vegetable oil

1/4 cup finely grated Parmesan cheese

pizza sauce, optional

Makes 3 Calzones. Each Calzone: 423 calories; 3 gm dietary fiber; less than 1 gm soluble fiber; 47 gm carbohydrates; 22 gm protein; 17 gm fat (35% calories from fat); 38 mg cholesterol; 654 mg sodium; 212 mg potassium; 434 mg calcium.

Vegetable Turnovers with Spinach Cheese Filling

These savory little packages make wonderful lunches or light suppers. The vegetable and cheese filling is nutritious and delicious. Make the entire recipe and freeze leftovers for impromptu snacks, lunchbox treats, or unexpected guests.

Dough

no stick cooking spray

1 package (5/16 ounce) HODGSON MILL ACTIVE DRY YEAST

1 cup HODGSON MILL OAT BRAN HOT CEREAL

2 to 2 1/2 cups HODGSON MILL UNBLEACHED FLOUR

1/2 teaspoon granulated sugar

1 teaspoon salt

2 egg whites

2 tablespoons vegetable oil

3/4 cup very warm water, 115° F.

Filling

1 tablespoon vegetable oil

1 small onion, chopped

2 cloves garlic, minced

Continued on next page

Spray a bowl with no stick cooking spray. In a medium-sized mixing bowl, blend the yeast with the oat bran hot cereal, 2 cups flour, sugar, and salt. With a wooden spoon, blend in egg whites, oil, and very warm water. Stir thoroughly, and continue to stir until all ingredients are well blended. Turn onto a floured board and knead to incorporate the remaining 1/2 cup flour. Knead until dough is smooth and satiny.

Place dough in the prepared bowl, turning to coat thoroughly. Cover and allow to rise in a warm, draft-free place for 30 minutes.

Meanwhile, prepare the filling. In a large skillet, heat oil. Sauté onion, and garlic until translucent. Add celery and spinach, a little at a time. Cover skillet, adding more spinach as it cooks down. Remove cover, and cook until all liquid has been absorbed. Sprinkle with oat bran hot cereal and stir to blend. Add cheeses and mix to blend and heat. Cool slightly, add salt and pepper to taste.

Preheat oven to 400 ° F. Spray a cookie sheet with no stick cooking spray.

Divide dough into 12 portions. On a floured board, roll each portion into a 5 inch round, about 1/8 inch thick. Fill half the circle with 1/3 cup filling. Fold over and seal edges with a fork. Brush with egg white.

Continued on next page

Vegetable Turnovers with Spinach Cheese Filling

Continued from previous page

Bake for 15 to 20 minutes until turnovers are browned. Serve with Dijon mustard on the side.

Makes 6 servings of 2 turnovers each. Each turnover: 187 calories; 3 gm dietary fiber; less than 1 gm soluble fiber; 26 gm carbohydrates; 7 gm protein; 6 gm fat (28% calories from fat); 5 mg cholesterol; 321 mg sodium; 297 mg potassium; 92 mg calcium.

Continued from previous page

Filling

2 ribs celery, sliced

1 pound spinach, rinsed 3 times to remove sand and tough stems

1/4 cup HODGSON MILL OAT BRAN HOT CEREAL

2 tablespoons freshly grated Parmesan cheese

1/4 cup Feta cheese, crumbled

1/2 cup lowfat cottage cheese

salt to taste

pepper to taste

1 egg white, beaten

Dijon mustard

Caribbean Meat Paté

Meat Paté is a traditional food of West Indians from the Virgin Islands. In this version, Mary has reduced the fat and cholesterol, increased the fiber, and preserved the distinctive island flavor. Meat Paté takes time to prepare, but it's time well spent. This is definitely an appetizer worthy of the most festive occasions.

Dough

1 1/2 to 2 cups
HODGSON MILL
UNBLEACHED FLOUR

1 cup HODGSON MILL
WHITE OR YELLOW
CORN MEAL

2 tablespoons sugar

1 teaspoon salt

1 egg

2 egg whites, beaten

5 tablespoons skim milk

Filling

2 tablespoons vegetable
oil

1 large onion, finely
chopped

1 cup celery, chopped

2 cloves garlic, minced

1 jalapeño pepper,
seeded and minced
(optional)

1 pound ground chicken
or turkey

3 tablespoons chili
powder

1 cup grated potato

1 cup chicken stock (or
water)

salt to taste

vegetable oil for frying

To make dough, place 1 1/2 cups flour, corn meal, sugar, and salt in a medium-sized bowl. Whip egg and egg whites lightly with milk. With a pastry blender, cut the egg mixture into flour mixture. Add more flour, if necessary, to make an elastic dough. Form dough into 20 balls.

To make the filling, heat 2 tablespoons vegetable oil in a large pan. Add onion, celery, garlic, jalapeño pepper, ground chicken or turkey, and chili powder. Sauté until the meat is well browned. Add potatoes and stock. Cover, and cook 10 more minutes. Drain meat and cool for 10 minutes. Salt to taste.

Heat vegetable oil in a deep fat fryer or in a heavy saucepan to 375° F.

Assemble paté on a floured board. Roll a dough ball as thin as possible—about 5 inches in diameter. Fill with 2 to 3 tablespoons of hot meat mixture. Fold dough over to make a half moon, and crimp edges with a fork. Repeat with the other dough balls and the remaining meat filling.

Place a few of the paté in a deep fat fryer basket. Lower into the fat and fry 3 to 4 minutes, until they are golden brown. Meat paté may be served immediately, or refrigerated and reheated in a 350° F. oven for 10 minutes. Cooked or uncooked paté may be frozen for up to 1 month.

Makes 10 servings of 2 paté each. Each serving: 295 calories; 1 gm dietary fiber; 1 gm soluble fiber; 29 gm carbohydrates; 21 gm protein; 10 gm fat (31% calories from fat); 21 mg cholesterol; 356 mg sodium; 324 mg potassium; 36 mg calcium.

Mini Turkey Burgers

Mary has created an interesting variation on the classic American burger. The crunchy, chewy buns are subtly flavored, with Parmesan cheese. Ground turkey, Monterey Jack cheese, cilantro, and oat bran blend to make a very tasty burger. Together, they're fun to nibble and easy to make.

In a medium-sized bowl, dissolve the yeast in the warm water.

Combine 1 cup oat bran hot cereal, flour, Parmesan cheese, salt, and oil until well blended. Add the yeast mixture and knead lightly until dough sticks together.

Spray another medium-sized bowl with no stick cooking spray. Put the mixture in a warm bowl, cover, and allow dough to rise in a warm, draft-free place for 30 minutes. After mixture has risen, knead dough again for 2 to 3 minutes, adding flour until dough is easy to handle.

Spray 2 large cookie sheets with no stick cooking spray. Between 2 layers of plastic wrap, roll out dough to 1/8 inch thick. Cut into 1 1/2 inch rounds (or other shapes) and arrange on cookie sheet, 2 inches apart. Cover and allow to rise in a warm, draft-free place for 15 minutes.

Preheat oven to 400 ° F. Bake buns for 8 to 10 minutes until well browned on tops and bottoms.

Spray a baking sheet with no stick cooking spray. Preheat broiler or charcoal grill. Blend turkey with cheese, cilantro, and remaining oat bran hot cereal. Form into 20 mini burgers. Broil for 5 minutes. Serve hot on buns.

Makes 20 burgers. Each: 65 calories; less than 1 gm dietary fiber; less than 1 gm soluble fiber; 6 gm carbohydrates; 3 gm protein; 3 gm fat (38% calories from fat); 5 mg cholesterol; 79 mg sodium; 29 mg potassium; 32 mg calcium.

Buns

1 package (5/16 ounce) HODGSON MILL ACTIVE DRY YEAST

1 cup very warm water, 115° F.

1 1/4 cups HODGSON MILL OAT BRAN HOT CEREAL

1 1/2 to 2 cups HODGSON MILL UNBLEACHED FLOUR

1/4 cup freshly grated Parmesan cheese

1 teaspoon salt

1/4 cup vegetable oil

no stick cooking spray

Burgers

1/2 pound ground turkey

4 ounces Monterey Jack cheese, shredded

1/4 cup finely chopped cilantro

Spring Rolls

The light, crisp dough complements the subtle flavors of the vegetables inside— sprouts, mushrooms, and peapods. Spring rolls take time to make but they are well worth it. Serve with hot mustard or plum sauce, a side of fried rice, and plenty of hot tea.

Dough

1 1/2 cups HODGSON MILL UNBLEACHED FLOUR

1/2 teaspoon salt

2 eggs, beaten until foamy

3/4 cup cold water

Filling

8 ounces shredded raw chicken

2 tablespoons soy sauce

1 egg white

1 tablespoon cornstarch

1 tablespoon olive oil

2 cups finely chopped vegetables (1/3 cup each scallions, mushrooms, bean sprouts, pea pods, celery, and bok choy)

2 cloves garlic, finely chopped

vegetable oil for frying

Place flour in a large mixing bowl. Add salt and make a well in center of the mixture. Add eggs, mixing well. Then add water, kneading mixture until it becomes soft. Turn onto a floured board and knead until smooth and elastic. Cover and allow to rest for 45 minutes.

To make filling, blend chicken with soy sauce, egg white, and cornstarch. Heat olive oil in a medium-sized pan. Quickly sauté chicken mixture and add vegetables. Cook until vegetables are very tender, and mixture is soft.

Turn spring roll dough onto floured board and divide into 8 pieces. With a rolling pin, roll until dough is very thin, almost transparent. Dust on both sides with flour and allow to stand for an additional 10 minutes to stiffen. Place 1/8 of vegetable mixture into the corner of each skin. Overlap sides, and roll tightly.

In a wok or other heavy pan, heat the vegetable oil to 375° F. Fry egg rolls until well browned, turning often, about 5 minutes.

Makes 8 servings. Each serving: 234 calories; 1 gm dietary fiber; less than 1 gm soluble fiber; 19 gm carbohydrates; 14 gm protein; 11 gm fat (43% calories from fat); 93 mg cholesterol; 428 mg sodium; 178 mg potassium; 25 mg calcium.

Muffuletta

In the mood for something zesty and tantalizingly different? Try this crusty round loaf of Italian bread filled with marinated vegetables, spicy meat, and tangy cheese. Southerners will recognize this as a New Orleans submarine sandwich.

Blend olives, celery, vegetables, oil, parsley, lemon juice, garlic, oregano, and pepper. Cover and refrigerate for 8 hours or overnight.

Spray a large bowl with no stick cooking spray. In a small bowl, blend yeast with 1 cup water and allow to rest for 5 minutes. Place 1 cup water with salt in a second large bowl. Add the yeast mixture. Blend 2 1/2 cups unbleached flour with HODGSON MILL BEST FOR BREAD WHITE FLOUR. Pour into yeast mixture, stirring into a thick dough.

Turn onto a floured board and knead the dough into a manageable ball, adding flour as necessary. Place dough in prepared bowl, turning to coat thoroughly. Cover with plastic wrap, then with a damp towel, and allow to rise in a warm, draft-free place for about 1 hour. The dough will almost double in bulk.

Spray a baking pan with no stick cooking spray. Turn the dough onto a floured bowl and knead down. Form into a 6 to 7 inch round. Put on prepared sheet, cover with plastic wrap, and allow to rise in a warm, draft-free place for 1 hour. Preheat the oven to 425° F. Bake for 35 to 45 minutes. Remove bread from sheet, put bread directly on rack, reduce oven temperature to 350 ° F., and allow bread to finish baking until golden brown, about 20 minutes.

To assemble sandwich, cut cooled loaf of bread in half horizontally. Drain olive mixture, reserving liquid. Brush the cut sides of bread with liquid. Layer bottom of loaf with sliced salami, half of the olive mixture, the provolone, the remaining olive mixture, and the ham. Top with lettuce leaves. Cover with top of bread. Cut into wedges to serve.

Makes 6 servings. Each serving: 466 calories; 2 gm dietary fiber; less than 1 gm soluble fiber; 47 gm carbohydrates; 17 gm protein; 24 gm fat (47% calories from fat); 28 mg cholesterol; 1327 mg sodium; 201 mg potassium; 153 mg calcium.

Stuffing

1/2 cup pimento stuffed olives, chopped

1/2 cup ripe olives, chopped

1/2 cup celery, chopped

1/2 cup mixed pickled vegetables, chopped

1/3 cup vegetable oil

1/4 cup parsley, chopped

3 tablespoons lemon juice

1 clove garlic, minced

1 tablespoon fresh oregano, chopped (or 1 teaspoon dried oregano)

freshly grated pepper

Bread

no stick cooking spray

1 package (5/16 ounce) HODGSON MILL ACTIVE DRY YEAST

2 cups warm water, 115° F.

1 teaspoon salt

3 cups HODGSON MILL UNBLEACHED FLOUR

1 cup HODGSON MILL BEST FOR BREAD WHITE FLOUR

Sandwich Filling

4 ounces thinly sliced salami

4 ounces sliced provolone cheese

4 ounces thinly sliced capacola or other ham

lettuce leaves for garnish

Pot Stickers

Prepare these pan-fried Chinese dumplings in advance and serve as an appetizer or as part of a classic Chinese meal. A bit of ginger, sherry, and soy sauce in the filling gives pot stickers an authentic flavor. They're also terrific with fresh chili dip.

Dumpling Mixture

2 cups HODGSON MILL UNBLEACHED FLOUR

1/2 cup cold water

3/4 cup boiling water

Filling Mixture

1/2 pound bok choy leaves

1/2 pound ground pork, cooked and drained

1 scallion, minced with tender green top

2 tablespoons dry sherry

2 teaspoons soy sauce

1/4 teaspoon ginger

Fresh Chili Dip

1/4 cup finely chopped red and green chili peppers

6 tablespoons soy sauce

2 tablespoons red wine vinegar

2 tablespoons sesame oil

1/2 cup vegetable oil for frying

Put 1 cup flour in a medium-sized mixing bowl and add cold water, blending well. Mix and knead into a soft dough. Place the second cup of water in a separate mixing bowl. Add boiling water gradually. Mix and knead into a soft dough. Blend doughs together and knead until elastic, but not sticky. Cover with a damp towel and allow to rest for 15 minutes.

Steam bok choy until tender. Mince, squeezing out excess water. Blend with pork, scallions, sherry, soy sauce, and sugar.

Roll dough into a long tube, about 1 inch in diameter. Divide into 18 portions. Flour each dumpling and roll into thin circle. Put about 1 tablespoon filling in the center of each dumpling. Moisten edges and pinch to seal. Repeat for 18 dumplings. Cover with a damp towel.

Make chili sauce by blending chili peppers with soy sauce and vinegar. Heat sesame oil and pour over all.

Meanwhile, put 2 tablespoons oil in a big skillet, distributing evenly over skillet surface. Place all pot stickers in the skillet and pour in cold water until it comes halfway up the sides of the pot stickers. Cover and heat to boiling. Cook for 3 minutes.

Remove skillet from heat and drain liquid. Rearrange pot stickers. Add remaining oil to the pan, being careful to distribute evenly. Cover pan and fry on low heat until the bottoms of the pot stickers are brown, about 10 minutes. (If pot stickers stick to the pan, they are not brown enough.)

Makes 18 pot stickers. Each pot sticker: 106 calories; less than 1 gm dietary fiber; less than 1 gm soluble fiber; 11 gm carbohydrates; 5 gm protein; 4 gm fat (35 % calories from fat); 10 mg cholesterol; 547 mg sodium; 114 mg potassium; 11 mg calcium.

Basic Pizza Recipe

This pizza crust recipe makes three all-American favorites: pizza, triple-decker pizza, and pepperoni bread.

Pizza Crust

HODGSON MILL OAT BRAN HOT CEREAL or HODGSON MILL OAT FLOUR in the pizza crust adds nutrition, makes a thin crispy crust, and lends a nut-like flavor. Or you may use all white or wheat flour.

In a food processor fitted with steel blade or in a blender, mill oat bran hot cereal until fine and flour-like, about 2 minutes.

Dissolve yeast in warm water. Allow to rest for 5 minutes. Stir in flour, sugar, salt, olive oil, and 1 cup oat bran hot cereal. Knead in remaining oat bran hot cereal by hand. This takes about 5 minutes; the dough will be smooth and elastic.

Spray a medium-sized bowl with no stick cooking spray. Place pizza dough in bowl and turn to coat thoroughly. Cover and allow to rise in a warm, draft-free place for 15 minutes. Spray one, 14 inch pizza pan or two, 10 inch pizza pans with no stick cooking spray. Stretch pizza crust to fit pan and flute outer edges of pizza dough to hold fillings.

Makes 8 servings. Each serving: 177 calories; 3 gm dietary fiber; 2 gm soluble fiber; 28 gm carbohydrates; 4 gm protein; 5 gm fat (25% calories from fat); 0 mg cholesterol; 123 mg sodium; 49 mg potassium; 5 mg calcium.

1 1/2 cups HODGSON MILL OAT BRAN HOT CEREAL or HODGSON MILL OAT BRAN FLOUR

1 package (5/16 ounce) HODGSON MILL ACTIVE DRY YEAST

1 cup very warm water, 115° F.

1 1/2 cups HODGSON MILL UNBLEACHED FLOUR

2 teaspoons granulated sugar

1/2 teaspoon salt

2 tablespoons olive oil

no stick cooking spray

"Bread gained by labour has a fine taste."
— *Italian Proverb*

Pizza Primavera

The secret of authentic Italian primavera sauce is using juicy, plump, very ripe tomatoes and fresh basil. Topped with a combination of mozzarella, provolone, and Parmesan cheese, this luscious sauce makes ordinary pizza extraordinary.

4 cups very ripe, chopped tomatoes

2 cloves garlic, sliced

1 tablespoon olive oil

2 tablespoons vegetable oil

2 tablespoons chopped fresh basil (or 2 teaspoons dry basil)

2 tablespoons chopped Italian parsley

salt and pepper to taste

One, 14-inch unbaked pizza crust (Page 125)

4 ounces mozzarella cheese, shredded

2 ounces provolone cheese, shredded

2 ounces Parmesan cheese, finely grated

Put tomatoes, garlic, oils, basil, and parsley in blender or food processor. Pulse until tomatoes are coarsely chopped. Salt and pepper to taste.

Preheat oven to 425 ° F.

Top pizza crust with primavera sauce. Sprinkle cheese evenly over sauce. Bake pizza for 18 to 20 minutes, until cheeses and crust are browned.

Makes 8 servings. Each serving: 329 calories; 4 gm dietary fiber; 2 gm soluble fiber; 32 gm carbohydrates; 13 gm protein; 16 gm fat (45% calories from fat); 19 mg cholesterol; 390 mg sodium; 219 mg potassium; 263 mg calcium.

"With bread all woes are sweet." — Italian Proverb

Triple Decker Pizza

Mary often serves this pizza extravaganza at her teenager's after-football parties. It's a dish for hearty appetites. Two generous layers of zesty Italian sausage, rich tomato sauce, and mozzarella cheese are topped with pizza crust. Watch it disappear!

Spray a baking sheet with no stick cooking spray.

Divide pizza dough into 3 parts. Roll the first part into a 9 x 7 inch rectangle and place on baking sheet. Place half of the sausage, half of the pizza sauce, and half of the cheese onto the rectangle.

Roll the second part slightly smaller than the first part. Put on top of the first part. Top with remaining sausage, sauce, and cheese.

Roll the third part slightly larger than the first part. Place over second part. Crimp and seal all 3 crusts. Allow pizza to rest in a warm place for 15 minutes. Preheat oven to 375° F.

Bake 25 to 30 minutes, until crust is well browned.

Makes 6 servings. Each serving: 482 calories; 4 gm dietary fiber; 2 gm soluble fiber; 43 gm carbohydrates; 22 gm protein; 23 gm fat (44% calories from fat) ; 51 mg cholesterol; 952 mg sodium; 380 mg potassium; 270 mg calcium.

no stick cooking spray

1 recipe Pizza Dough (page 125)

1/2 pound hot Italian sausage, cooked, drained, and crumbled

1 cup pizza or tomato sauce (homemade or prepared)

8 ounces mozzarella cheese, shredded

"He who has hunger has no bread; who has bread has no hunger."
— Italian Proverb

Pepperoni Bread

Mary's aerobics instructor once served pepperoni bread as an after-class snack. Since then, Mary has become an avid fan of this zany treat. It blends the pungent flavor of pepperoni and homemade bread. Try it grilled with herb butter for the picnic crowd.

no stick cooking spray

3 tablespoons extra virgin olive oil

3 cloves garlic, chopped

1/2 recipe Pizza Dough (page 125)

4 ounces freshly grated Parmesan cheese

6 ounces sliced pepperoni

Spray a baking sheet with no stick cooking spray.

In a small frying pan, heat olive oil with garlic over low heat. Allow garlic to steep in hot oil without browning.

On a floured board, roll pizza dough into a 12 x 9 inch rectangle. Transfer to prepared baking sheet. Brush olive oil and garlic mixture over rectangle. Sprinkle Parmesan cheese over olive oil mixture, keeping it within 1 inch of all edges. Distribute pepperoni evenly over cheese.

Starting from the longer side, roll tightly. Turn seam side down, turning under edges to seal pizza roll. Cover and place in a warm, draft-free place for 15 minutes.

Preheat oven to 400 ° F. Bake 25 to 30 minutes, until well browned.

Makes 8 servings. Each serving: 391 calories; 3 gm dietary fiber; 2 gm soluble fiber; 30 gm carbohydrates; 14 gm protein; 23 gm fat (55% calories from fat); 11 mg cholesterol; 820 mg sodium; 135 mg potassium; 206 mg calcium.

"He who has a trade will find bread everywhere."
— Italian Proverb

Reuben Rolls

This sandwich might not look like a Reuben, but it certainly tastes like one. Thousand Island Dressing, sauerkraut, corned beef, and Swiss cheese are all rolled into a loaf of delicious, caraway rye bread. Mary enjoys serving it cold as an accompaniment to a crisp summer salad. It's also terrific with a bowl of hot soup in the winter.

Spray a large bowl with no stick cooking spray.

In another mixing bowl, blend 1 cup white flour with the HODGSON MILL BEST FOR BREAD WHITE FLOUR, rye flour, salt, and yeast. Stir thoroughly with a wooden spoon. Add oil, caraway seed, and very warm water. Continue to stir until all ingredients are well blended. Dough will be stiff. Turn onto a floured board and knead in enough of the remaining flour to make dough smooth and satiny. This takes about 10 minutes. Dough may also be mixed and kneaded in a food processor or in a mixer with a dough hook.

Place dough in prepared bowl, turning to coat all sides thoroughly. Cover with plastic wrap and allow to rise in a warm, draft-free place for 1 hour. The dough will be warm, light, and almost doubled in bulk.

Spray a large cookie sheet with no stick cooking spray.

Knead down dough and divide into 2 balls. On a well floured surface, roll the first part into a into a 9 x 12 inch rectangle. Spread half the Thousand Island Dressing on the rectangle, keeping it 1 inch away from all four sides. Sprinkle half sauerkraut atop Thousand Island Dressing. Next, put half of the corned beef slices on top of sauerkraut, and half the Swiss cheese slices on top of the corned beef. Carefully roll sandwich up, keeping fillings inside dough as tightly as possible. The roll should be 12 inches long and about 3 inches wide. Put on prepared cookie sheet seam side down. Repeat for second Reuben Roll.

Continued on next page

Dough

1 1/2 cups HODGSON MILL UNBLEACHED FLOUR

1/2 cup HODGSON MILL BEST FOR BREAD WHITE FLOUR

1 1/2 cup HODGSON MILL RYE FLOUR

1/2 teaspoon salt

1 package (5/16 ounce) HODGSON MILL ACTIVE DRY YEAST

2 tablespoons vegetable oil

1 tablespoon caraway seed

1 1/4 cups very warm water, 115° F.

Filling

3 tablespoons Thousand Island Dressing

1 1/2 cups sauerkraut, rinsed and drained

8 ounces sliced corned beef

6 ounces Swiss cheese, thinly sliced

Reuben Rolls

Continued from previous page

Make sure all edges of the rolls are sealed, and the ends of the rolls are folded under. Cover with plastic wrap, and allow to rise in a warm, draft- free place for 30 more minutes. Preheat oven to 350° F. Brush with beaten egg white. Bake for 35 to 40 minutes or until roll is well browned. Serve hot, room temperature, or cold.

Makes 2 rolls, 12 servings. Each serving: 131 calories; less than 1 gm dietary fiber; less than 1 gm soluble fiber; 14 gm carbohydrates; 7 gm protein; 5 gm fat (37% calories from fat); 15 mg cholesterol; 266 mg sodium; 65 mg potassium; 79 mg calcium.

Cornish Pasties

This traditional English dish is hearty enough to serve for dinner to meat-and-potato lovers, yet portable enough to put in a lunch box. Lean beef, onions, carrots, and potatoes are wrapped in light pastry dough and baked until golden brown. Delicious hot or cold, served with a pungent mustard.

Spray a large bowl with no stick cooking spray.

To prepare pastry: in a medium-sized mixing bowl, blend yeast with oat bran hot cereal, 2 cups flour, sugar, and salt. With a wooden spoon, blend in egg whites, oil, and very warm water. Stir thoroughly, and continue to stir until all ingredients are well blended. Turn onto a floured board and knead to incorporate the remaining 1/2 cup flour. Knead until dough is smooth and satiny, about 10 minutes. The dough may be mixed and kneaded in a food processor or an electric mixer with a dough hook.

Place dough in the prepared bowl, turning to coat thoroughly. Cover, and allow to rise in a warm, draft-free place for 30 minutes.

To prepare filling, cut beef into 1/2 inch pieces, discarding all fat. Toss beef with onions, potatoes, and carrots.

Divide dough into 6 portions. On a floured board, roll each portion into a 9 inch round, about 1/8 inch thick.

Preheat oven to 375° F. Place about 1 cup filling onto half of each circle. Moisten the edge of each circle with water. Fold over and press edges to seal. Cut slits in top of each pastie. Brush with milk. Bake until crust is golden brown, about 50 to 55 minutes.

Makes 6 pasties. Each pastie: 499 calories; 5 gm dietary fiber; 3 gm soluble fiber; 60 gm carbohydrates; 32 gm protein; 13 gm fat (24% calories from fat); 64 mg cholesterol; 403 mg sodium; 687 mg potassium; 39 mg calcium.

Pastry

1 package (5/16 ounce) HODGSON MILL ACTIVE DRY YEAST

1 cup HODGSON MILL OAT BRAN HOT CEREAL

2 to 2 1/2 cups HODGSON MILL UNBLEACHED FLOUR

1/2 teaspoon granulated sugar

1 teaspoon salt

2 egg whites

2 tablespoons vegetable oil

3/4 cup very warm water, 115° F.

Filling

1 pound cooked lean beef, such as round steak or well-trimmed chuck roast

2 medium onions, chopped

2 large potatoes, cooked and cubed with skins

1 cup carrots, cooked and diced

salt to taste

freshly ground pepper

skimmed milk

hot mustard (optional)

Buns

1/2 cup HODGSON MILL BULGUR WHEAT

1 cup boiling water

1 package (5/16 ounce) HODGSON MILL ACTIVE DRY YEAST

1/2 cup very warm water, 115° F.

2 to 2 1/2 cups HODGSON MILL UNBLEACHED FLOUR

1 cup HODGSON MILL BEST FOR BREAD WHITE FLOUR

1/4 cup freshly grated Parmesan cheese

1 teaspoon salt

2 tablespoons vegetable oil

All-Vegetable Filling

3/4 to 1 pound firm tofu

1/4 cup salad dressing

1 tablespoon Dijon mustard

1 tablespoon soy sauce (or 1 tablespoon Worcestershire sauce)

1 clove garlic, minced

1 rib celery, chopped

1/2 teaspoon tumeric

1 tablespoon fresh chopped dill weed (or 1 teaspoon dried dill)

1/2 cup carrot, grated

3 scallions, minced

salt to taste

freshly ground pepper

lettuce and tomato for garnish

STUFFED BREADS

Bulgur Buns with All-Vegetable Stuffing

HODGSON MILL BULGUR WHEAT WITH SOY GRITS is a new food product blended for extra nutrition, nutty texture, and a unique taste. Stuffed with a delicious, all-vegetable filling of tofu, carrots, celery, scallions, and garlic, these buns will please vegetarians and non-vegetarians alike.

Soak bulgur wheat in boiling water for 15 minutes.

In a medium-sized bowl, dissolve yeast in warm water.

Combine bulgur wheat, 2 cups unbleached flour, and HODGSON MILL BEST FOR BREAD WHITE FLOUR with Parmesan cheese, salt, and oil until well blended. Add the yeast mixture and knead lightly, until dough sticks together.

Spray another medium-sized bowl with no stick cooking spray. Put the mixture in a warm bowl, turning to coat thoroughly. Cover, and allow dough to rise in a warm, draft-free place for 30 minutes. After mixture has risen, knead dough again for 2 to 3 minutes, adding flour until dough is easy to handle.

Spray 2 large cookie sheets with no stick cooking spray. Between 2 layers of plastic wrap, roll out dough to 1/8 inch thick. Cut into 1 1/2 inch rounds (or other shapes) and arrange on cookie sheet, 2 inches apart. Cover and allow to rise in a warm, draft-free place for 15 minutes.

Preheat oven to 400° F. Bake buns for 8 to 10 minutes, until well browned on tops and bottoms. Cool and split buns.

Drain tofu. In a medium-sized bowl, mash the tofu with a fork. Add salad dressing, mustard, and seasonings. Add vegetables and lightly mix again. Chill. Salt and pepper to taste, and serve on buns. Top with lettuce and tomato.

Makes 12 stuffed buns. Each bun: 150 calories; less than 1 gm dietary fiber; less than 1 gm soluble fiber; 21 gm carbohydrates; 8 gm protein; 4 gm fat (23% calories from fat); 3 mg cholesterol; 307 mg sodium; 95 mg potassium; 83 mg calcium.

HISTORICAL BREAD TIDBITS

- Bread played a part in medieval social hierarchy. Only royalty ate fresh-baked bread; nobles were allowed day-old loaves; gentry, two-day-old loaves; and scholars and clerics, three-day-old loaves. The remaining populace was subjected to four-day-old bread.

- George Washington was a bread miller of international reputation, and Abraham Lincoln earned his nickname, Honest Abe, while working for a miller.

- The official seal of New York State includes a windmill and two flour barrels, symbols of New York's importance as a milling center in colonial times.

Recipes for bread featured on the previous page are:
Wheat-Wheat-Wheat Bread, Page 142
Hot Jalapeño Bread, Page 145
Corn Meal Herb Bread, Page 147

CHAPTER 8

BREAD MAKER BREADS
by Mary Ward

Recipes included in this chapter are:

Imagine waking up to the aroma of freshly baked bread. What a wonderful way to start your day! With an electric bread maker, this pleasant fantasy can become a reality. All you do is measure ingredients into the container, set the timer, and *voilá,* a few hours later you have a loaf of homemade bread. The machine mixes, kneads, and lets the dough rise, all automatically! Electric bread makers are available from Panasonic, National, Well Built, Dak and other manufacturers. Retailers say that consumers are never disappointed with these appliances and never return them.

This is not surprising; making bread the automatic way is fun, easy, and almost foolproof. If you follow directions to the letter you'll always get perfectly delicious bread.

Bread makers do have some limitations, however. With some machines, the loaves are much smaller than those you make by hand. If you use all purpose flour, bread flour, or unbleached flour, the loaf may rise so high that individual slices may need to be cut in half. Recipes that use whole grain flour yield smaller, more compact loaves.

Bread makers are perfect for people who love fresh, wholesome, nutritious bread, but just don't have the time to make it the old-fashioned way.

Here are some tips for successful baking with an automatic bread maker.

• Read instructions for your machine carefully, and follow them exactly.

• Pack flour into the measuring cup so there are no air pockets.

- Always use 1/2 to 1 package of HODGSON MILL ACTIVE DRY YEAST. It is potent and yields a large, light loaf.

- Use no more than the recommended amount of flour for each loaf.

- Once you set the machine, leave it alone. Don't change settings during the bread making cycle.

- Use 2 to 2 1/4 cups of any variety of flour (4 to 4 1/2 cups for the larger machines). We recommend that at least half of this flour be HODGSON MILL UNBLEACHED FLOUR, which is high in gluten and produces well-formed loaves.

- We suggest using 1/2 to 1 cup HODGSON MILL BEST FOR BREAD WHITE FLOUR in combination with HODGSON MILL UNBLEACHED FLOUR. If you do this, your bread will have a fine texture and a strong cell wall. This will enable you to add tasty fillings and whole grain flours to your bread maker breads. There are so many wonderful varieties of flour to choose from. Experiment with HODGSON MILL RYE FLOUR, HODGSON MILL WHOLE WHEAT FLOUR, HODGSON MILL OAT BRAN HOT CEREAL, HODGSON MILL OAT BRAN FLOUR, HODGSON MILL BUCKWHEAT FLOUR, HODGSON MILL CORN MEAL, HODGSON MILL CRACKED WHEAT, HODGSON MILL WHEAT BRAN, and HODGSON MILL BULGUR WHEAT WITH SOY GRITS.

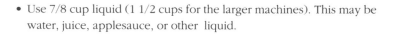

- Use 7/8 cup liquid (1 1/2 cups for the larger machines). This may be water, juice, applesauce, or other liquid.

- Use 1/4 cup dry skimmed milk (1/2 cup for larger machines). This adds calcium as well as flavor to your breads. We do not recommend using fresh milk in the electric bread maker.

- Use 1 teaspoon salt (2 teaspoons for larger machines) for a lighter loaf and better crumb.

- Use 1 teaspoon to 1 tablespoon sugar or other sweetener, such as maple syrup, brown sugar, or honey for a fine crumb and light loaf.

- Use 1 tablespoon vegetable oil (2 tablespoons for larger machines) to bring out the flavor and texture of the bread. We recommend soft margarine for delicate, sweet breads; vegetable oil, such as corn, safflower, or canola oil for hearty breads; and extra virgin olive oil for ethnic breads.

- To give bread distinctive flavor and texture, add 2 to 4 tablespoons chopped herbs, fruits, vegetables, raisins or nuts. Try adding 2 to 4 tablespoons grated Parmesan, cheddar, or Romano cheese.

- Read the recipe book that comes with your machine thoroughly. Then read the recipes in *Blue Ribbon Breads*. Now, you're ready to create your own recipes.

- To adapt a recipe for an automatic bread maker, cut down the flour to 2 cups (3 or 4 cups for the larger machines), the yeast to 1 to 2 teaspoons, and all other ingredients, proportionally. Almost any yeast bread recipe can be adapted to the bread maker. The possibilities are endless. After you've used your bread maker for a while, you'll invent some tempting combinations of your own. Here are a few of our favorite bread maker recipes.

White Bread

There's nothing quite as satisfying and comforting as basic white bread. This recipe makes a firm loaf with a fine crumb. White Bread makes wonderful toast and excellent sandwiches. It tastes just as good in the morning with a cup of coffee as it does in the afternoon with a cup of tea.

1 1/2 cups HODGSON MILL UNBLEACHED FLOUR

1/2 cup HODGSON MILL BEST FOR BREAD WHITE FLOUR

2 tablespoons sugar

1 teaspoon salt

1 tablespoon margarine

1 tablespoon dry milk

7/8 cup water

1 package (5/16 ounce) HODGSON MILL ACTIVE DRY YEAST

Attach kneading blade and put all ingredients, except yeast, into the bread pan.

Close the top lid. Add the yeast to yeast dispenser. Set timer and start button. When beeper sounds, carefully remove bread from pan and cool on wire rack.

Makes 1 loaf, 8 slices. Each slice: 137 calories; less than 1 gm dietary fiber; less than 1 gm soluble fiber; 26 gm carbohydrates; 4 gm protein; 2 gm fat (13% calories from fat); less than mg cholesterol; 270 mg sodium; 62 mg potassium; 16 mg calcium.

"Never fall out with your bread and butter."
— English Proverb

Oat Bran Bread

A light, fiber-rich, nutritious loaf. Serve toasted at breakfast with marmalade or fruit spread. A delightful way to start your morning.

Attach kneading blade and put all ingredients, except yeast, into the bread pan.

Close the top lid. Add the yeast to yeast dispenser. Set timer and press the start button. When beeper sounds, carefully remove bread from pan and cool on wire rack.

Makes 1 loaf, 8 slices. Each slice: 147 calories; 1 gm dietary fiber; less than 1 gm soluble fiber; 27 gm carbohydrates; 4 gm protein; 2 gm fat (13% calories from fat); less than 1 mg cholesterol; 268 mg sodium; 62 mg potassium; 16 mg calcium.

1 1/2 cups HODGSON MILL UNBLEACHED FLOUR

1/2 cup HODGSON MILL BEST FOR BREAD WHITE FLOUR

4 tablespoons HODGSON MILL OAT BRAN HOT CEREAL

2 tablespoons sugar

1 tablespoon margarine

1 tablespoon dry milk

1 teaspoon salt

7/8 cup water

1 package (5/16 ounce) HODGSON MILL ACTIVE DRY YEAST

"Without dish and without bread, there is no good company."
— French Proverb

Oat Bran Flour Nutri-Bread

Every morsel of this bread is packed with nutrition. It's made with unbleached flour, wheat germ, and oat bran flour, which has a rich, nutty flavor. Serve toasted to fully savor the delicate taste.

1 1/2 cups HODGSON MILL UNBLEACHED FLOUR

1/2 cup HODGSON MILL BEST FOR BREAD WHITE FLOUR

1/4 cup HODGSON MILL OAT FLOUR

1 tablespoon HODGSON MILL WHEAT GERM

2 tablespoons sugar

1 tablespoon dry milk

1 tablespoon margarine

1 teaspoon salt

7/8 cup water

1 package (5/16 ounce) HODGSON MILL ACTIVE DRY YEAST

Attach kneading blade and put all ingredients, except yeast, into the bread pan.

Close the top lid. Add the yeast to yeast dispenser. Set timer and press the start button. When beeper sounds, carefully remove bread from pan and cool on wire rack.

Makes 1 loaf, 8 slices. Each slice: 153 calories; 1 gm dietary fiber; less than 1 gm soluble fiber; 29 gm carbohydrates; 4 gm protein; 2 gm fat (12% calories from fat); 1 mg cholesterol; 268 mg sodium; 74 mg potassium; 17 mg calcium.

"He who has good flour makes good bread."
— Italian Proverb

Hearty Rye Bread

A dense bread that's chewy and flavorful. Makes a memorable corned beef sandwich that's a meal in itself. Or serve Hearty Rye Bread hot with soup or stews.

Attach kneading blade and put all ingredients, except yeast, into the bread pan.

Close the top lid. Add the yeast to yeast dispenser. Set timer and press the start button. When beeper sounds, carefully remove bread from pan and cool on wire rack.

Makes 1 loaf, 8 slices. Each slice: 142 calories; less than 1 gm dietary fiber; less than 1 gm soluble fiber; 27 gm carbohydrates; 4 gm protein; 2 gm fat (14% calories from fat); 1 mg cholesterol; 292 mg sodium; 97 mg potassium; 27 mg calcium.

1 1/4 cups HODGSON MILL UNBLEACHED FLOUR

1/2 cup HODGSON MILL BEST FOR BREAD WHITE FLOUR

1/2 cup HODGSON MILL RYE FLOUR

2 tablespoons sugar

1 tablespoon dry milk

1 tablespoon margarine

1 teaspoon salt

7/8 cup water

2 tablespoons caraway seed

2 tablespoons drained sauerkraut

1 package (5/16 ounce) HODGSON MILL ACTIVE DRY YEAST

"He is content again with his own bread."
— German Proverb

Wheat-Wheat-Wheat Bread

Using 50/50 flour ensures that your whole wheat bread will be substantial, but not heavy. You'll love the crunchy texture and the nutty, whole grain taste of this bread.

1 1/2 cups HODGSON MILL 50/50 FLOUR

1/2 cup HODGSON MILL BEST FOR BREAD WHITE FLOUR

2 tablespoons HODGSON MILL CRACKED WHEAT CEREAL*

2 tablespoons HODGSON MILL WHEAT GERM

2 tablespoons honey

1 tablespoon butter or margarine

1 tablespoon dry milk

1 teaspoon salt

7/8 cup water*

1 package (5/16 ounce) HODGSON MILL ACTIVE DRY YEAST

Attach kneading blade and put all ingredients, except yeast, into the bread pan.

*For a less crunchy loaf, soak the cracked wheat in 1/4 cup boiling water for 5 minutes. Decrease the water in the recipe to 5/8 cup.

Close the top lid. Add the yeast to yeast dispenser. Set timer and press the start button. When beeper sounds, carefully remove bread from pan and cool on wire rack.

Makes 1 loaf, 8 slices. Each slice: 140 calories; 2 gm dietary fiber; less than 1 gm soluble fiber; 27 gm carbohydrates; 4 gm protein; 2 gm fat (13% calories from fat); 1 mg cholesterol; 284 mg sodium; 111 mg potassium; 21 mg calcium.

"Who wants better bread than wheaten wants too much." — Italian Proverb

Buckwheat Bread

Just a touch of nutritious buckwheat flour gives this loaf a distinctive, tangy flavor. Simpler than pancakes for breakfast, buckwheat bread can be served toasted, with cream cheese, fruit spread, or cinnamon sugar.

Attach kneading blade and put all ingredients, except yeast, into the bread pan.

Close the top lid. Add the yeast to yeast dispenser. Set timer and press the start button. When beeper sounds, carefully remove bread from pan and cool on wire rack.

Makes 1 loaf, 8 slices. Each slice: 140 calories; 1 gm dietary fiber; less than 1 gm soluble fiber; 26 gm carbohydrates; 4 gm protein; 2 gm fat (13 % calories from fat); less than 1 mg cholesterol; 268 mg sodium; 72 mg potassium; 17 mg calcium.

1 1/2 cups HODGSON MILL UNBLEACHED FLOUR

1/2 cup HODGSON MILL BEST FOR BREAD WHITE FLOUR

1/4 cup HODGSON MILL BUCKWHEAT FLOUR

2 teaspoons sugar

1 tablespoon dry milk

1 tablespoon margarine

1 teaspoon salt

7/8 cup water

1 package (5/16 ounce) HODGSON MILL ACTIVE DRY YEAST

"Without bread and salt, the gathering is not complete."
— Russian Proverb

Cheese Bread

Needless to say, this bread makes terrific ham sandwiches. Serve hot with Dijon mustard. Make cheese bread with Parmesan, then experiment with Cheddar, Monterey Jack, or Romano. They're all delicious.

1 1/2 cups HODGSON MILL 50/50 FLOUR

1/2 cup HODGSON MILL BEST FOR BREAD WHITE FLOUR

3 tablespoons Parmesan cheese, grated

2 tablespoons sugar

1 tablespoon dry milk

1 teaspoon salt

1 tablespoon margarine

7/8 cup water

1 package (5/16 ounce) HODGSON MILL ACTIVE DRY YEAST

Attach kneading blade and put all ingredients, except yeast, into the bread pan.

Close the top lid. Add the yeast to yeast dispenser. Set timer and press the start button. When beeper sounds, carefully remove bread from pan and cool on wire rack.

Makes 1 loaf, 8 slices. Each slice: 145 calories; 2 gm dietary fiber; less than 1 gm soluble fiber; 26 gm carbohydrates; 5 gm protein; 3 gm fat (17% calories from fat); 3 mg cholesterol; 67 mg sodium; 107 mg potassium; 51 mg calcium.

"Skill and learning bring bread and honor."
— Danish Proverb

Hot Jalapeño Bread

Warning—this bread is really hot! Use fewer jalapeños for a milder bread. It makes deliciously unusual sandwiches. The wild, spicy flavor contrasts well with cheese and cucumbers, cold roast beef, and chicken. Have a pitcher of iced tea handy!

Attach kneading blade and put all ingredients, except yeast, into the bread pan.

Close the top lid. Add the yeast to yeast dispenser. Set timer and press the start button. When beeper sounds, carefully remove bread from pan and cool on wire rack.

Makes 1 loaf, 8 slices. Each slice: 138 calories; less than 1 gm dietary fiber; less than 1 gm soluble fiber; 23 gm carbohydrates; 5 gm protein; 2 gm fat (16% calories from fat); 0 mg cholesterol; 314 mg sodium; 44 mg potassium; 59 mg calcium.

1 cup HODGSON MILL UNBLEACHED FLOUR

1 cup HODGSON MILL BEST FOR BREAD WHITE FLOUR

2 tablespoons (or less) chopped jalapeño peppers

7/8 cup water

1/4 cup shredded Monterey Jack cheese

1 tablespoon sugar

1 teaspoon salt

1 package (5/16 ounce) HODGSON MILL ACTIVE DRY YEAST

"A loaf with love is better than a fowl with sorrow."
— Italian Proverb

Rye Tomato Bread

Here's a nice change from rye bread. Simply use tomato juice or vegetable juice for the liquid. This tangy, tasty bread makes great sandwiches—especially when they include cheese. It adds a festive touch to soups and winter casseroles, too.

1 cup HODGSON MILL BEST FOR BREAD WHITE FLOUR

3/4 cup HODGSON MILL UNBLEACHED FLOUR

1/2 cup HODGSON MILL RYE FLOUR

7/8 cup tomato juice or vegetable juice

1 tablespoon sugar

1 teaspoon salt

1 tablespoon vegetable oil

1 tablespoon caraway seed

1/4 cup chopped tomato

1 package (5/16 ounce) HODGSON MILL ACTIVE DRY YEAST

Attach kneading blade and put all ingredients, except yeast, into the bread pan.

Close the top lid. Add the yeast to yeast dispenser. Set timer and press the start button. When beeper sounds, carefully remove bread from pan and cool on wire rack.

Makes 1 loaf, 8 slices. Each slice: 215 calories; less than 1 gm dietary fiber; less than 1 gm soluble fiber; 43 gm carbohydrates; 7 gm protein; 2 gm fat (10% calories from fat); 0 mg cholesterol; 331 mg sodium; 110 mg potassium; 12 mg calcium.

"Much bread grows in a winter night."
— English Proverb

Corn Meal Herb Bread

You'll like the crunchy texture of the corn meal in the top crust. The herbs create a wonderful fragrance while it's baking and a spectacular taste once it's done. Serve warm with sweet butter.

Attach kneading blade and put all ingredients, except yeast, into the bread pan.

Close the top lid. Add the yeast to yeast dispenser. Set timer and press the start button. When beeper sounds, carefully remove bread from pan and cool on wire rack.

Makes 1 loaf, 8 slices. Each slice: 141 calories; less than 1 gm dietary fiber; less than 1 gm soluble fiber; 26 gm carbohydrates; 4 gm protein; 2 gm fat (14% calories from fat); 0 mg cholesterol; 246 mg sodium; 67 mg potassium; 9 mg calcium.

1 cup HODGSON MILL UNBLEACHED FLOUR

3/4 cup HODGSON MILL BEST FOR BREAD WHITE FLOUR

1/2 cup HODGSON MILL WHITE OR YELLOW CORN MEAL

4 tablespoons fresh, chopped herbs (chives, cilantro, Italian parsley, and basil) or 4 teaspoons dry herbs

1 tablespoon vegetable oil

7/8 cup water

1 teaspoon salt

1 tablespoon sugar

1 package (5/16 ounce) HODGSON MILL ACTIVE DRY YEAST

"Here is bread, which strengthens man's heart, and is therefore called the staff of life."
— Matthew Henry

Glazed
Cinnamon Bread

Enjoy the lovely aroma of this bread while it's baking and the sweet, spicy taste when it's done. Serve hot, as a desert bread or for a fancy brunch. The perfect companion for fresh fruit and poached eggs.

Dough

1 1/2 cups HODGSON MILL UNBLEACHED FLOUR

1/2 cup HODGSON MILL BEST FOR BREAD WHITE FLOUR

1 tablespoon cinnamon

2 tablespoons sugar

1 tablespoon margarine

1 teaspoon salt

1 tablespoon dry milk

7/8 cup water

1 package (5/16 ounce) HODGSON MILL ACTIVE DRY YEAST

Glaze

1/2 cup confectioners sugar

2 teaspoons milk

Attach kneading blade and put all ingredients except yeast, sugar, and milk into the bread pan.

Close the top lid. Add the yeast to yeast dispenser. Set timer and press the start button. When beeper sounds, carefully remove bread from pan and cool on wire rack.

Blend confectioners sugar with milk. Drizzle over loaf.

Makes 1 loaf, 8 slices. Each slice: 164 calories; 1 gm dietary fiber; less than 1 gm soluble fiber; 33 gm carbohydrates; 4 gm protein; 2 gm fat (11% calories from fat); less than 1 mg cholesterol; 269 mg sodium; 69 mg potassium; 28 mg calcium.

Buckwheat Applesauce Bread

This hearty bread has a coarse crumb and slightly sweet flavor. It's wonderful toasted, for a real stick-to-the ribs breakfast. Serve with fruit and cheese for a light lunch.

Attach kneading blade and put all ingredients, except yeast, into the bread pan.

Close the top lid. Add the yeast to yeast dispenser. Set timer and press the start button. When beeper sounds, carefully remove bread from pan and cool on wire rack.

Makes 1 loaf, 8 slices. Each slice: 125 calories; less than 1 gm dietary fiber; less than 1 gm soluble fiber; 23 gm carbohydrates; 3 gm protein; 2 gm fat (14% calories from fat); 0 mg cholesterol; 245 mg sodium; 56 mg potassium; 5 mg calcium.

1 cup HODGSON MILL UNBLEACHED FLOUR

3/4 cup HODGSON MILL BEST FOR BREAD WHITE FLOUR

1/4 cup HODGSON MILL BUCKWHEAT FLOUR

1/2 cup applesauce

1/2 cup water

1 tablespoon vegetable oil

1 teaspoon salt

1 package (5/16 ounce) HODGSON MILL ACTIVE DRY YEAST

"Good fellowship is half bread." — Italian Proverb

Whole Wheat Dinner Rolls

Your bread maker can prepare dough for rolls, bagels, and baguettes, too. You'll want to try them all, but we suggest you start with Mary's favorite recipe for whole wheat rolls. Serve warm with butter.

1 1/2 cups HODGSON MILL 50/50 FLOUR

1/2 cup HODGSON MILL BEST FOR BREAD WHITE FLOUR

3 tablespoons sugar

2 tablespoons dry milk

1 teaspoon salt

4 tablespoons margarine

1 egg

1/2 cup water

1 teaspoon HODGSON MILL ACTIVE DRY YEAST

1 egg, beaten for brushing tops of rolls

Place the kneading blade in the bread pan. Add all ingredients except yeast. Insert pan securely into cavity. Close the top lid. Fill yeast dispenser with dry yeast.

Select dough setting, and press the start button. When the beeper sounds, place the dough in a greased bowl; cover with plastic wrap and let rest for 20 minutes. Divide into 12 balls. Let rest for 10 minutes. Roll each ball into a wedge shape, approximately 1/4 inch thick. Starting with the widest side, roll up the wedge loosely towards the point.

Place on a greased baking pan with the point downwards. Shape rolls into a crescent shape. Cover with a damp cloth and let rise until almost doubled, about 30 minutes.

Brush rolls with beaten egg. Bake at 375° F. for 10 to 15 minutes, until rolls are a deep golden brown. Remove from pan immediately.

Makes 12 rolls, each roll: 135 calories; 2 gm dietary fiber; less than 1 gm soluble fiber; 18 gm carbohydrates; 4 gm protein; 5 gm fat (35% calories from fat); 47 mg cholesterol; 231 mg sodium; 88 mg potassium; 25 mg calcium.

Bulgur Bread

HODGSON MILL BULGUR WHEAT WITH SOY GRITS is a new product that has been blended for high nutrition and quality taste. Mary likes to use a little in breads. The combination of bulgur and soy adds crunch as well as great flavor. The aroma of this bread is wonderful, and so is the taste!

Soak bulgur wheat in boiling water for 5 minutes.

Attach kneading blade and put softened bulgur wheat with all ingredients, except yeast, into the bread pan.

Close the top lid. Add the yeast to yeast dispenser. Set timer and press the start button. When beeper sounds, carefully remove bread from pan and cool on wire rack.

Makes 1 loaf, 8 slices. Each slice: 136 calories; 2 gm dietary fiber; less than 1 gm soluble fiber; 26 gm carbohydrates; 4 gm protein; 2 gm fat (13% calories from fat); 1 mg cholesterol; 284 mg sodium; 111 mg potassium; 21 mg calcium.

1/4 cup HODGSON MILL BULGUR WHEAT WITH SOY GRITS

1/4 cup boiling water

1 1/4 cups HODGSON MILL 50/50 FLOUR

1/2 cup HODGSON MILL BEST FOR BREAD WHITE FLOUR

2 tablespoons honey

1 tablespoon vegetable oil

1 tablespoon dry milk

1 teaspoon salt

3/4 cup water

1 package (5/16 ounce) HODGSON MILL ACTIVE DRY YEAST

"Happy are they who find their bread already baked."
— *Scottish Proverb*

Adapting recipes for electric bread makers

Most of Carol's yeast bread recipes can be adapted for use in an electric bread maker. Bread makers come in 2 cup and 4 cup sizes. Most of Carol's recipes are for 8 cups of flour or grain products. To adapt her recipes, then, for a 2 cup bread maker, simply use 1/4 of the ingredients. For example, here is her recipe for White Bread (page 28) with the electric bread maker version. To clarify the comparison, the order of ingredients for Carol's White Bread has been changed.

White Bread	**Electric Bread Maker White Bread**
8 cups unbleached flour	2 cups unbleached flour
1/2 cup sugar	2 tablespoons sugar
1 teaspoon salt	1/4 teaspoon salt
1/2 cup margarine, melted	2 tablespoons margarine, melted
2 1/2 cups lukewarm water	7/8 cup lukewarm water
2 packages yeast	1 teaspoon yeast
1 beaten egg	

Pack flour, sugar, salt, margarine, and water in bread maker. Add yeast to yeast dispenser cup.

When adapting Carol's recipes for the electric bread maker:
- Load flour and grains into the bread pan first. Pack down with a spoon. Add liquid ingredients last. Then, load yeast into yeast dispenser cup.
- In recipes where Carol soaks or softens, add softened ingredients to bread pan last.
- If you want to eliminate the egg, add 1 teaspoon margarine.
- Use a total of 7/8 cup liquid (for a 2 cup bread maker) and no more than 2 1/2 cups flour or grain (for a 2 cup bread maker).

BREAD: A baked dough, raised by yeast or some other leavening, made with any of a variety of milled grains. Some of the gases produced by the leavening are trapped in the dough, causing it to expand. The pores containing these gases are made permanent by heat. Only dough that includes wheat or rye flour has the ability to retain these gases and rise.

WHOLE GRAIN WHEAT: Wheat is a grain seed made up of three parts: the starchy endosperm that makes white flour when milled, the germ, and the seed husk, known as bran. The whole grain is the entire wheat kernel. Whole wheat products are brown and more nutritious than white flour products. Hard wheats have more gluten than soft wheats and are better suited to making bread.

GLUTEN: The stretchy protein, present primarily in wheat flour, that interacts with leavening and causes the dough to rise, giving bread its familiar texture.

LEAVENING: The substance that ferments the dough and causes it to rise. Yeast, the most widely used leavening, is a living plant whose spores float in the air. Early breads were probably leavened with the yeast formed in barley and millet beer and with wild yeast spores. Regular bread baking encourages the growth of yeast in the air of your kitchen. The more bread you bake, the better each batch will rise. HODGSON MILL ACTIVE DRY YEAST is a heavy-duty yeast, perfect for use in whole grain bread.

RISING: The period during which the yeast works and releases tiny carbon dioxide bubbles, causing the dough to swell.

KNEAD: Working the bread dough, usually with the hands, to mix the yeast cells throughout the dough and to achieve the required smoothness and elasticity.

KNEADING DOWN: The second kneading of the dough, when air bubbles are literally kneaded out. If dough is not properly kneaded down, the finished loaf is full of holes.

PROOFING: The second rising of bread dough, after it has been kneaded down and shaped.

INDEX

INDEX